CONT

CATEGO

BEACHES 'N' SWIMMING HOLES 5
BOATING & CANOEING 7
CLASSIC CHURCHES 9
FISHING 12
HIKING AND BIKING 13
HISTORIC HOMES AND HOTELS 15
TROPICAL ISLANDS 19
LIGHTHOUSES AND FORTS 21
MUSEUMS 23
NATURE PRESERVES 26
OLD STEAMBOAT LANDINGS 27
PARKS WITH PIZZAZZ 30
RESTORED HISTORIC DISTRICTS 32
RIVER TOWNS 33
SCENIC DRIVES 36
SEAFOOD "A LA" APALACHICOLA 38
SOMEPLACE DIFFERENT 40
APALACHICOLA ANNUAL FESTIVALS & EVENTS 47
HISTORIC HOMES GUIDE 49
FUN SITE MAPS 54-62
RIVER MILEAGES & LANDINGS 63-64

CATEGORIES

BEACHES 'N' SWIMMING HOLES Pg. 5

1. Salinas Park Beach 5
2. Gulf Front Or Bayshore 5
3. Sunland's Rish Beach Park 6
4. Bon-Ton Swimming And Camping 6
5. 9 Miles Of Splish-Splash 6

BOATING & CANOEING Pg. 7

1. Drive Through Cypress Trees . . .7
2. Owl Creek To Bloody Bluff Paddle .7
3. Scott's Ferry 8
4. Pine Log Creek To Crooked River 9

CLASSIC CHURCHES Pg. 9

1. St. Patrick's 1929 9
2. First Baptist Church 1904 10
3. Florida's 6th Oldest Church 1838 10
4. St. Paul's AME 1913 11
5. Up From The Ashes 1901 11

FISHING Pg. 12

1. Bob Sikes Cut 12
2. Hickory Landing 12
3. Magnolia Lodge Landing 13

HIKING AND BIKING Pg. 13

1. Dune Ridges & Beach Hiking . .13
2. Bloody Bluff Cycle 14
3. A Bike-Hike In Tate's Hell 14

HISTORIC HOMES AND HOTELS Pg. 15

1. Gray House And History 1865 .15
2. Raney House 1834 16
3. Magnolia Hall 1838 16
4. Flatauer House 1908 17
5. Brigitte's Romantic Retreat . . .17
6. Town Landmark 1907 Inn 18
7. Coombs House Inn 1905 18

TROPICAL ISLANDS Pg. 19

1. St. George Island 19
2. Florida River Island 19
3. 600 pound Deer & Red Wolves 20
4. The Cape 20

LIGHTHOUSES AND FORTS Pg. 21

1. Stormy Cape — A Tippy Lighthouse 21
2. Move It Or Lose It Lighthouse 22
3. The Negro Fort 22
4. Crooked River Lighthouse 1894 23

MUSEUMS Pg. 23

1. Largest Estuarine Reserve In America 23
2. Apalachicola Maritime Museum 24
3. "Cruise" The Museum— 1877 Gov. Stone 24
4. "Cool It" 25
5. St. Vincent Visitor's Center . . .25

NATURE PRESERVES Pg. 26

1. Living In The Fast Lane Or New "Island" Home 26
2. Wilderness Preserve & Dune Ridges 26

OLD STEAMBOAT LANDINGS Pg. 27

1. Era of Stern-Side & Paddlewheelers 27
2. Howard Creek 27
3. Bryant Landing 28
4. Douglas Landing 28
5. Willis Lodge 28
6. Cotton Landing 29
7. The River Styx 29

PARKS WITH PIZZAZZ Pg. 30

1. Lafayette Park 1832 30
2. Picnics Beside I.C.W. 30
3. Chapman Botanical Gardens 31
4. Apalachicola River Wayside Park 31

RESTORED HISTORIC DISTRICTS Pg. 32

1. 40 Blocks Of Restoration 32
2. Commercial & Maritime Historic District 33

RIVER TOWNS Pg. 33

1. White City 33
2. Polly Parrot-Historic Sites & Tyrene's 34
3. Sopchoppy, "You've Come A Long Way Baby" 35
4. Town In A Time Capsule 35

SCENIC DRIVES Pg. 36

1. Yent Bayou Shore Drive 10 Miles 36
2. Indian Pass And Beach Driving 37
3. Creeks & Bayous Byway 37

SEAFOOD "A LA" APALACHICOLA Pg. 38

1. Meet & Eat The Royal Family 38
2. South's Best Seafood Eating . .39
3. Seafood-2-Go Market Districts 39

SOMEPLACE DIFFERENT Pg. 40

1. Scipio Creek Shrimp Fleet 40
2. Old St. Joseph Cemetery 1835 40
3. A Choice Place 41
4. "Ole" 10-Foot Hole At City Marina 42
5. Apalachicola Anchors— The Story 42
6. Catching Argopecten Irradians Concentricus 43
7. Chestnut Hill Cemetery 1832 43
8. River "King," Apalachicola 106 Miles 44
9. Moonrise—Sunset Pier 44
10. Fort Coombs Armory 1901 . . .45
11. Rainbow On A River 46
12. Twisty Red Oak River Fun . . .46

APALACHICOLA ANNUAL FESTIVALS & EVENTS Pg. 47

1. Florida's Oldest Seafood Fest .47
2. Historic Tour Of Apalachicola Homes 48
3. Gibson Inn Antique Car Road Race 48
4. Largest Chili Cook-Off 48
5. St. Vincent Island N.W.R. Tram Tour 48

HISTORIC HOMES GUIDE Pg. 49

1. City Historic District Map 49
2. Style Guides 50-53

FUN SITE MAPS Pg.

1. Florida River Island 54
2. Apalachicola River Basin 55
3. St. Vincent National Wildlife Refuge 56
4. St. George Island State Park 57
5. Cape St. George State Preserve 57
6. Apalachee Savannahs Scenic Byway 58
7. Wilderness Preserve 59
8. Apalachicola River Wildlife Environmental Area . . .60
9. Tate's Hell W.M.A. West Area 61
10. Old Steamboat Landings 62

RIVER MILEAGES & LANDINGS Pg. 63-64

SALINAS PARK BEACH

If I blinked I'd have missed this diamond-in-the-rough. A narrow sand entry drive opens into an extensive dune ridge and pinewoods area on a *stunning cove* of CAPE SAN BLAS. Park is about 60 acres having 10 picnic shelters (some grills), playground equipment and an octagonal OVERLOOK GAZEBO perched on the highest dune (30 ft.) Four dune boardwalks protect tall wavy sea oats and beach morning glories. Gulf bathing is relaxing because the *long curve* of beach cove gives protection on 3 sides from bumpity waves! Another unusual feature . . . . You may park your car next to your lunch shelter. Loggerhead sea turtles sometimes lay their eggs on the shore in mid-summer. You may need bug spray. One mile south of Salinas Park is historic marker for Confederate Saltworks where now stands beach vacation spot called OLD SALTWORKS CABINS & STORE (a nifty little place) ! ! !

Cape San Blas, FL   Rd 30-E   North of Fire Station
Open Daily   904-227-1223   Old Saltworks Cabins 904-229-6097

GULF FRONT OR BAYSIDE

A 6 mile peninsula of 2,516 acres with heavy forest that *supports deer!* A variety of water depth 40 ft to exposed sand bars creates hues of blues and greens. Gulf swimmers enjoy roomy beaches crowned by striking dune forms . . . . bayside gleaming sands lead out to grass flats where summer SCALLOPING is #1. Full facility picnic areas overlook ST. JOE BAY. Two bayside *hike trails* are "easy going" walks of 45 min. each. A car bridge spans pretty Eagle Harbor Lagoon where a rest bench aids perfect viewing of bird species. Campsites (119) are lush with greenery, shade and privacy----you may rent a Trout, Snapper, Scallop, Fish, Conch, Mackerel or Porpoise (not to ride) but to sleep in. These are the names of 8 lovely bayfront *cabins* perched on dunes. Boat Ramp is popular with fisherman and jet ski craft that go popping about the bay like ("hot-footed water-bugs") ! ! ! CANOE R-E-N-T-A-L-S available.

St. Joseph Peninsula State Park   Near Cape San Blas West
on Rd 30-E (9 Mi)
Open Daily 8-Sunset   904-227-1327

SUNLAND'S RISH BEACH PARK

Waving sea oats anchor *100 acres* of dunes and bayfront natural areas. Dunes are cross-hatched by wide boardwalks leading to aqua Gulf waters and a TUNNEL passes under busy Rd 30-E to wooded bayfront. Only Florida residents with HANDICAPPING conditions may rent the spacious fully equipped octagonal cottages or dorms. There are *miles of ramp & boardwalks* connecting beaches, cottages, Olympic-size swim pool, a huge event hall with large FIREPLACE, a miniature golf course and a shuffle board court. Acres on bayside have nature trails for critter or bird watching. "Billy Joe" Rish Park is tucked into beautiful Cape San Blas and has all amenities completely handicap access ! ! !

Cape San Blas Fl   Rd 30-E   Open Year Round
Reservations   Sunland Center At Marianna
8-4:30 Mon-Fri   904-482-9221

BON-TON SWIMMING AND CAMPING

A high (30 ft) grassy hill overlooks deep WRIGHT LAKE. Chunky trunked slender CYPRESS ring the lake. Tables and grills afford view to see your "kiddos" water antics and still do your cook-thing by the fire ! ! ! I loved aroma of turpentine and berry bushes floating out of the woods. C-A-M-P AREA (very upscale) with 1st class facilities . . . . Wright Lake renovation completed in 1996! Sort of an outdoor Holiday Inn! Hunt up "ole house place' (south) of picnic ground where a Cypress Wood Factory once operated. A tiny landing lets to the river. If you like to "photo" Cypress Trees you could "overdose" here ! ! ! An Interpretive Walk Trail threads through the woods. Nearby (.3 Mi) is HICKORY LANDING.

Sumatra Fl Rd   65 (2 Mi) South Go (West) Forest Rd 101
(2 Mi) Dirt
Open Daily   Apalachicola Nat'l Forest Wright Lake   904-926-3561

9 MILES OF SPLISH-SPLASH

St. George Island State Park is where you bring all your floating toys, sun screen and yummy-whoppers. A "skinny" (wide point 1.5 miles) sand spit of 1,962 acres fulfills all daydreams. Frolic in Gulf of Mexico or "Apalach" Bay. Watch frequent fly-bys as park is near migratory flyways in Spring & Fall . . . . Other "stuff" to do . . . . ??? Yup . . . . You'll find 'em ! ! ! Map Pg 57

Eastpoint Fl   Off Hwy 98 Take Causeway to East End of Island
S.G.I. State Park 904-927-2111
Open Daily   CAMPING

BOATING & CANOEING

DRIVE THROUGH CYPRESS TREES

Age is 500 to 1,000 year. Their girth is wide enough to drive a small car through . . . . They are living ! ! ! February is best month to locate the giants as feathery leaves are absent then. We approached through East River Cutoff where 3 land fingers poke north making it easy to spot more regal Cypress (less old). Near "Thank-You-Ma'am" creek on high banks (5 ft) is a pine to break all records (about 16 ft round). Pass the creek about 200 ft. It's on west side (100 yds) in. I used a small power boat but canoeing is the best way to enjoy these languid back-bayou waters . . . . Base of Cypress trunks form natural "sculpture" with no 2 alike! The Redwood-like-Cypress must be Florida "CHAMPS"----Look for them on East River (west side) about 1 1/2 miles north of Caesar Creek (east bank)----you won't believe your "peepers" ! ! ! Map Pg 55

Apalachicola Fl   Directions Above

OWL CREEK TO BLOODY BLUFF PADDLE

I put in at Hickory Landing on Owl Creek. A 2 mile slough is lined with 250 year old Cypress with trunks forming lifelike natural *sculpture forms*! Wildlife?? Not much. Superb beauty?? Absolutely. Look for tangled Tupelo roots resembling human forms or hollow Cypress trunks cut long ago that look like old-time 5 foot wooden wash tubs. On entering the river, stay close to shore as current makes easier paddling. First large island (south) is Brickyard Island which can be explored if water levels allow. Many trees along river-bank have high water flood marks well over 15 ft ! ! ! Heard plenty of bird chatter heading south to FT GADSDEN STATE HISTORIC SITE. Do stop at the high banks (old steamboat landing) to see the Interpretive Center, Cemetery and dirt berms of old 1814 British Post . . . . Restrooms and picnic shelter, too! We took out at Bloody

Bluff which is a quite large island. I was unable to find the *Bloody Bluff Cemetery* but did not spend much time on the effort. Dirt road to Hwy 65 is a lovely drive. Map Pg 62

- Hickory Landing to River 2 Miles
- Owl Creek Mouth to Ft Gadsden 4 Miles
- Ft Gadsden to Bloody Bluff 7 Miles

Apalachicola Fl (East) to Rd 65 & North to Apalachicola National Forest Rd 101 (Hickory Landing)
Open Daily Nat'l. Forest 904-926-3561
Adventures In Paradise 904-653-8463
Jeanni's Journeys 904-927-3259

SCOTT'S FERRY

Before 1900 a ferryman rode folks, wagons and produce from bank to bank . . . I spoke with a woman at the general store whose mother was a regular rider on the ferry! A bridge now spans the 200-300 feet old ferry site. You've heard of 5-Diamond Hotels ? ? ? Scott's Ferry hugs up to *a 5-Diamond River, THE CHIPOLA!* First thing to take your eye on these green riverbank acres is a lifesize SCULPTURE OF A BLACK BEAR (circa 1920). CAMPGROUND is spacious, green & shady----Sheltered picnic tables-yup! Excellent boat ramp, also used by Canoers and Water Bikers. S.F. is at south end of Chipola's 52 mile run. Of the 36 canoe trails in Florida, Chipola is most U-N-U-S-U-A-L . . . . because of limestone bluffs, cave system (north), hardwoods of beech, magnolia, dogwoods and 400 year old oaks ! ! ! Most paddling is "a piece of cake". Some shoals are tricky (for experts). Others downright dangerous like the shoal nicknamed, LOOK & TREMBLE FALLS below bridge over S.R. 274----At times portage is needed. I've seen much wildlife including playful beaver. If you work up a hunger save time for chowing down at Scott Ferry's MINNIE LEE'S RESTAURANT ! ! !

Scott's Ferry Fl (45 Miles North of Apalachicola) Rd 71 (N.W. Side of Bridge)
Open Daily CANOE RENTAL & CAMPING
Scott's Ferry General Store & Campground 904-674-2900

PINE LOG CREEK TO CROOKED RIVER

A remote mysterious silent back-water. It is also deep and splendidly S-C-E-N-I-C ! ! ! Banks can be 100 to 25 feet across. Creek flows through wet habitat with healthy stands of hardwood bottom forests. Oak and Cypress dominate languid side sloughs. I especially enjoyed the frequent twists and turns and mirror forest reflections while paddling. In summer you pass armies of 5 inch white Marsh Mallows, (not for eating) these are swamp flowers. Energetic boaters canoe east through Crooked River to the bridge at Hwy 319 which spans OCHLOCKONEE RIVER----I prefer to lay back in the back-waters. Pack plenty of film water and grub.

Carrabelle Fl *North on Hwy 67 (8-10 Mi) Put-In at JIM ODOM BRIDGE Park 100 Ft North of Bridge. West Side is Paved, Pull Off & Ramp for Canoes and Small Boats*
Open Daily

CLASSIC CHURCHES

ST PATRICK'S 1929

Style is Romanesque. Main entrance framed by recessed arches and ornate stonework. Just above rests a 6 foot circular many hued stained glass creation that filters rainbow colors to church interior. North and South Buttresses balance the high ceilinged structure. Earth-tint tiles lend roofing a Spanish character. Front facade is dominated by statue of (who else)? St Pat with shamrock Bishop's Miter and Staff. Church interior will delight those who wish a return to the "Traditional Catholic Church" before Pope John "opened" all the doors & windows ! ! ! Inside is highly decorative confessional, round brass chandeliers suspended above wood pews. Back and front altars support the old, friendly (tried & true) statues of SAINTS we grew up with----St Francis, St Joseph, Blessed Virgin Mary, Sacred Heart, St "Paddy", Infant of Prague, Martin De Porres and St Theresa. Peek around several support pillars to admire a minimum of 20 arching stained glass windows. Exterior belfry adds beauty and music!

Apalachicola Fl *Corner Ave C & 6th St*
Open Sunday *904-653-9453*

FIRST BAPTIST CHURCH 1904

Main door still retains its original brass lock fixture. On entering you immediately focus on the THEATRE IN THE ROUND architecture with floor sloping to the sanctuary. *Ceiling is stunning*. It was constructed by skilled craftsmen. The whole is done in close fit long wooden strips in geometric patterns of slants squares & intricately cut designs. Below on interior walls is brightly polished and veneered wainscotting. Under sanctuary floor was a surprise----the old deep baptism pool, no longer used----Southeast corner of church leans on a 3 section white wood tower with arches & turrets resembling an eastern prayer tower . . . . A tall pointy steeple once sat here but was destroyed years ago . . . . I like the "new look". On north, south and east exterior walls 3 multihued GOTHIC WINDOWS draw your attention. They are large occupying most of each wall space. To appreciate their rainbow spectrums, best viewing is from inside. Outdoors on northeast corner are picnic tables under Pecan. Oak and Sycamore trees.

Apalachicola Fl   9th St & Ave D
Open Sunday   904-653-9540

FLORIDA'S 6TH OLDEST CHURCH 1838

White pine church was pre-fabricated in White Plains, NY and built with wooden pins. Double hand worked entrance columns indicate GREEK REVIVAL style. Ornate wood ceiling is curved to sides and stencils (never repainted) are in reds, gold and blues ! ! ! Interior highlights are dark wood wainscotting, sanctuary recessed paneling that is duplicated in the ceiling and richly colored windows depicting Holy Family & Apostles. I was much taken with the rare 1840's ANTIQUE ORGAN. It is a Henry Erben Tracker organ. Attached near keyboard is a *brass dish candle holder* for reading music at night programs! Notice the old-world "scroll" lettering on various organ stops. TRINITY EPISCOPAL CHURCH is on the National Historic Register. Outdoors under an oak is a skillfully crafted quite decorative wrought-iron rest bench. Two other buildings are on grounds. A Rectory-1900 and Benedict Hall-1932.

Apalachicola Fl   Trinity Episcopal Church
Gorrie Square Hwy 98 & 6th St
Open Daily   904-653-9550

UP FROM THE ASHES 1901

Original 1846 house of worship had a sanctuary fire which ruined the church and almost decimated the whole town. Over 70 buildings went up in the 1900 conflagration. New sanctuary was complete in 1901 at cost of $3,500. FIRST UNITED METHODIST CHURCH stands like a tall white lightbeam on the town's main street. There are 18 gothic windows and a few smaller circular ones. Motif focus is on nature. Inside they cast glorious hues! Skilled artisans crafted the wood ceiling, shining communion railing and other interior appointments. Original belfry ladder is still in use. Lighting glows from fluted fixtures and a large central chandelier. I counted 25 pipes on the organ ! ! ! Wooden church exterior walls have "turned and carved" decorations replicating gothic window theme. You'll admire peaked roof ornaments and finials on belfry tower.

Apalachicola Fl *First United Methodist Church*
Hwy 98 & 5th St
Open Sunday *904-653-9530*

ST PAUL AFRICAN METHODIST EPISCOPAL 1913

Church is an imposing handsome red brick structure. Front facade focus is on peaked Gothic windows. Entry is via double wooden doors at base of (2) east and west brick towers. Both are crowned by tall metal steeples. Stained glass artistry graces 10 smaller 7 foot window panels. Much larger stained glass creations dominate 3 walls (south, east & west). *These were made in Germany* specially for St Paul's. Sunlight casts striking hues of blues, greens and yellows. Interior floor is graduated sloping to front. Modest glass globes and brass fixtures provide light. Construction took (8 years). It was completed in 1921. Since then there have been 2 fires and 2 reconstructions . . . . Continued "preservation" is aim of this small but determined congregation. St Paul A.M.E. enjoys listing on the NATIONAL REGISTRATION OF HISTORIC PLACES ! ! !

Apalachicola Fl *St Paul African Methodist Episcopal*
6th St & I Ave
Open Sunday *904-653-9454*

FISHING

BOB SIKES CUT

In 1950 Bob Sikes (Florida's original He-Coon) helped get the western third of St George Island cut off from the main island affording boats a direct path to the mainland and Apalachicola River. The corridor joins the bay and gulf and is one of Florida's fishing "hot spots". Long granite rock jetties (bay side) lead to clear gulf water. Bobbing boats haul back catches of Grouper, Trout, King Macks, Blues, Snapper, Angelfish and scads more "fin & scales" types ! ! ! A marvy place to take the family even if mom and kids hate fishing----Here's why----sparkling white sandy shores border both sides of the cut. This is where you beach your non-fishing folks with toys & yummys. Eureka! you are free to get with the more "serious & reel" program of stocking the fish cooler. You need a boat for access to Sikes Cut . . . . Aside from rewarding catches this gulf inlet is probably the most S-C-E-N-I-C in Florida (no development) ! ! ! Map pg 57

Apalachicola Fl 5 Mi South Across Bay (West End St George Island) Boat Access Only
Rentals Boss Charters Rainbow Marina 904-653-8139

HICKORY LANDING

Bass, Bream, Catfish is what folks had in their coolers. Small boat ramp is popular for easy launching and because it is on backwater, Owl Creek where fishing is good. The landing is a lovely green scene with 10 campsites on a circle snuggled up to the creekbank. You may picnic. Facility for toilet & drinking water. Some ground fires. Area is engulfed in Cypress and Hickory groves . . . . Owl Creek (2 Miles) has access to APALACHICOLA RIVER. Ramp is a *favorite with canoers* who enjoy OWL CREEK'S remote still waters and lavish display of unsettled "back-country" ! ! ! Map pg 62

Sumatra Fl Rd 65 South (2 Mi) Forest Rd 101 West (2.5 Mi)
Open Daily Camping Allowed
Apalachicola Nat'l Forest 904-926-3561

MAGNOLIA LODGE LANDING

On a high bluff (50 ft), possible old Indian Midden, you look down on mid-point of 75,000 acre, Dead Lakes. This "natural formation" occurred when Apalachicola River levees blocked normal flow of Chipola River. Shoals developed with high back-up water killing 12 miles of "gran-daddy" Cypress, which still stand----1 of the state's most "photographed sites" ! ! ! Lodge has almost 50 year history. Choose cabins, motel, triplex, duplex or small apartment----All squeaky clean. Folks were showing off Bass and Shellcrackers but my attention was on roses, hanging flower baskets and "Senator" Magnolia. Rockers on porches let you view all "goings-on" below on decks & docks. Magnolia Lodge Bluff is used by Tyndall Air Force navigators as a reference point. I watched (from my rocker) a "Snag Boat" with split hull. It pulls up Dead Head Cypress (sunk). This "pecky-wood" Cypress is popular as finished wood. I was happy as a clam just rockin' 'n' lookin'. I bet anglers think they died and went to "Heaven" ! ! !

Wewahitchka Fl (5 Mi North) On Rd 71
Open Daily Magnolia Lodge 904-639-5212

HIKING AND BIKING

DUNE RIDGES & BEACH HIKING

Morning of my hike was soggier than bread pudding so I left camera bike camcorder tripods and hiked the island of my dreams anyway. So much for 8 years planning. Dressed in Hefty Bag trash sacks we boated 1,000 ft from Indian Pass to ST VINCENT ISLAND. It is 9 miles long by 4 wide. No "2-leggers" live here, only deer, 'gator, hog and wolves (only 2) . . . . a breeding program. We "squish-squished" on Cabin Rd to the interior at Rd D which was hi-n-dri. Walking the spine of this ancient dune ridge it was hard to imagine that only 5,000 years ago this is where beach waves washed ashore. By noon a welcome sun appeared and we saw several of 10 habitats on St Vincent. Some were mixed hardwoods of Oak and Magnolia, Scrub Oaks, Wetlands and pure stands of Cabbage Palm. Harder walking but most awesome was our *shore walk* where beach dunes wear a crown of sturdy LIVE OAK. North & South roads have some shade overhang! Roads are well marked---- East, West are lettered----North, South roads are numbers. There are 80 miles of sand roads and 14 miles of beach . . . . TAKE WATER & GRUB ! ! ! I'd go back in a heartbeat . . . or a "raindrop" ! Map Pg 56

Apalachicola Fl Hwy 30 at Indian Pass Open Daily
St Vincent N.W.R. 904-653-8808
Daylight Hours Boat Access Only

BLOODY BLUFF CYCLE
2.3 Miles One-Way

Local lore recounts honor duels and vicious fights over women having occurred on B.B. Island. Bluff is now part of APALACHICOLA RIVER WILDLIFE & ENVIRONMENTAL AREA (50,458) acres. Bike path is a 2-track with green center strip. After mile 1 you have *several choices of side roads* to tour. Here forest become varied being a "combo" of upland hardwoods and low bottomland----See acres of BAY TREES which in Spring are covered with milk-white 5 inch magnolia-like flowers ! ! ! A pleasant picture in late summer were tall purple butterfly peas and tall yellow blooms I failed to identify. Closer to river the road CANOPIES for cool summer riding but you need "weapons-of-choice" for mean yellow flies. At mile 2.2 are remains of a wood cabin and brick chimney. Road ends at river site which in 1830's was a bustling steamboat landing . . . . A small boat ramp still exists. BLOODY BLUFF CEMETERY is nearby but daylight ran out on me so no time to search----I'll be back ! ! ! Map Pg 60

Apalachicola Fl Rd 98 (East 10 Mi) North on Rd 65 (12-15 Mi)
West on Bloody Bluff Rd At A.R. Wildlife
Environmental (SIGN)
Open Daily FIsh & Game Comm 904-265-3676

A BIKE-HIKE IN TATE'S HELL

A diverse 67,000 acre tract trying to live down a bad "rep". Donkey years ago a gent, Tate, got lost in the backwood swamps and after several days U-Turns, hunger and Condor-size mosquito attacks he slogged back to civilization . . . . When friends asked where he had been he answered, "To Hell And Back". Today you'd have to exert effort to get lost as roads are *well signed*. I never even had to pull out my compass or pink tie-strings. DEEP CREEK ROAD is entrance. Within 1/2 mile follow BUCKS SIDING RD. It has lots curves, though map shows it straight. Hike-Bike path is a high dry 2 track. Some canals on both sides chock full of lily blooms. Late summer we admired a multi-covered wildflower bonanza. Near mile 2 tall bushy CEDARS become common. Heavy forest garnished our trail to both sides. Frequently a licorice aroma floated from the woods with extensive stands of blooming Ti-Ti trees??? Countless side roads (2 Tracks) offer choices for other treks----we stuck with Buck Siding Rd for its beauty----An occasional "washout" is usually passable. On nearing WHISKEY GEORGE CREEK BRIDGE you encounter more wildlife ! ! ! Creekside camping is allowed but primitive is not my "thing" so we scampered back to our cozy digs in Apalachicola. Map Pg 61

Apalachicola Fl East On Hwy 98 (9 Mi) North On Rd 65 (13 Mi)
East On Deep Creek Rd to Buck Siding Rd
Open Year Round Fl Fish & Game 904-265-3676

HISTORIC HOMES AND HOTELS

GRAY HOUSE AND HISTORY 1865

This home is *not yet restored*. I believe past owners' history of 131 years make it *significant*. After the Civil War life was tough. Edwin Gray, a mullet fisherman, salvaged 342 hogshead of crude rum from a wrecked ship. He began a tavern trade in a conestoga wagon on an empty lot. With profits he built GRAY HOUSE. With wife and 17 children he lived here 26 years when he met death in a "bordello" shoot-out at the hands of W.A. Chestnut. Son, "Gentleman Jim" Gray, got the home in 1891. He exported cypress and added gables to the roof which are still there. In 1909 Jim died of cirrhosis and passed the house to son, Patrick. He was smitten by Samantha "Two High" Isbicki. He lost business and sanity dying by his own hand. Patrick's daughter, Lisa Gray, received ownership 1925. She wed her 1st cousin which scandalized the town. She passed ownership in 1927 to "Dapper Denny". He and his wife never lived in Apalach until hard times in 1929 when they returned from Paris. They couldn't abide the town's "uncouth populace" so sold to James Gray in 1930. He was a respected bookkeeper by day and illicit *still operator* by night. Business ties were in Chicago where he perished with mobster Chapelioni in a gangland execution in 1937. By 1954 Gray House passed to Myrtle Gray known for her superior baking skills and yummy pastries. She was loved by all and died at 89 years in 1981. Her son, Thomas Gray, is the current resident. Locally known as Capt. Tom who operates Adventures In Paradise (Boat trips to barrier islands, harbor tours, canoe trips).

Apalachicola Fl 5th St & Ave C (S.E. Corner) Gray House (Private)
Adventures In Paradise 904-653-8463

RANEY HOUSE 1834

Original construction was a simple building in the Federal Style. Before the Civil War in 1850 the home was "gussied-up" in Greek Revival and now stands as a *2-story 4 column home with portico*. The wooden home has tall window shutters and 8 fireplaces. A gigantic Magnolia tree shades the home and wide white picket fencing borders the yard. Some original furnishings still remain. Hanging chandeliers, an organ, dining room and other period pieces complete the interior. There were 8 Raney children with one becoming a Florida Supreme Court Justice. Raney's home was a political and social hub----He promoted the city's (short-lived) race track and provided a theater for circuit theatrical companies ! ! ! Raney House narrowly missed being burned by Union forces in 1863. It is now on the NATIONAL HISTORIC REGISTER.

Apalachicola Fl Corner Market St & Ave F
Open Sat 1-4 C of C 904-653-9419

MAGNOLIA HALL 1838

The area had no skilled carpenters so Thomas Orman had his massive hilltop "plantation" home cut to measure in New York. In 1838 it was assembled with pegs and looked down on the bustling steamboat harbor below. Orman planted sugar and rice on nearby OWL CREEK where 36 slaves worked his plantation. In 1994 after 44 years of neglect the 2 story home was restored and stands today in its former grandeur. In 1994 a union CIVIL WAR UNIFORM was found in a trunk ! ! ! Home is Pre-Victorian Greek Revival. There are 6 fireplaces (now gas), wrap-around porches, shuttered windows and period furniture----I loved *the bedroom 4-posters*. One was massive Empire Style Mahogany. Magnolia Hall is a GUESTHOUSE of most extraordinary high-style----Bedrooms are largest most ornate I've ever seen ! ! ! Hilltop site occupies about 4 acres. Formal rose garden invites strollers. For the more active there is a pool. Magnolia Hall is not the usual B. & B. I thought it unique, the perfect get-a-way to celebrate a "special time" in your life ! ! !

Apalachicola Fl 177 5th St Open Year Round
Magnolia Hall Guesthouse Reservations 904-653-2431

FLATAUER HOUSE 1908

Large families require large homes. Adolf Flatauer had both. He was a German Jewish merchant who chose the most elegant materials in building his imposing Apalachicola home. Main rooms (8) are 17 by 17 ft each with own glazed tile fireplace, mantle and bay window. Downstairs Library and Dining Room have dark wood sliding double doors. "Dead Head" Cypress was used extensively in the lower central hall area. Staircase is embellished with skilled wooden portiere work and scrolled brackets. In a 1980 restoration the roof received custom cut wood shingles. To replicate the home's original look, walk around 2 story porches and widow's walk were renovated. About 900 balusters (spindles) were made for porch railings. Notice the Capitals (decorative tops) on outside columns. Flatauer House is now home to GULF STATE BANK which sponsored the restoration. The bank is justly proud of returning this FREE CLASSIC STYLE home to its former grandeur. During regular hours they graciously WELCOME VISITORS.

Apalachicola Fl Ave E (Hwy 98) & 6th St
Open Mon-Fri 9-3 904-653-2126

BRIGITTE'S ROMANTIC RETREAT

This newly restored *Bed & Breakfast* is a charming 2 story wooden home built in 1915. Style is VICTORIAN SEASIDE. Behind the front yard rose garden a wrap-around porch looks enticing with its comfy rockers. Official greeter is Einstein who enjoys good conversation----Don't be intimated----He is a "parrot" ! All rooms are awash in ANTIQUES, some over 250 years old. Collection is eclectic and includes furniture, chandeliers, Rosewood wardrobes and s-o-o-o much more. The owners spent a lifetime accumulating their treasure from all around the globe. I was charmed with a rare Corn Merchant's Desk (a mobile office). Note exquisite fireplace tiles and you'll fall-in-love (perhaps again) in the elaborate HONEYMOON ROOM ! ! ! Old world hospitality is the "norm" at Brigitte's.

Apalachicola Fl   101 E. 6th St   904-653-3270
Bed & Breakfast   Open Year Round

TOWN LANDMARK 1907 INN

Like a richly set wedding banquet with 3 tiered cake, so appears 3 story GIBSON INN (the town center piece). Architecture is Victorian. Lobby walls, staircase and floors are cypress and heart pine. Each of 31 guestrooms is *appointed in its own style*. There are four-posters, clawfoot baths, antique armoires, and opulent period furnishings. Gibson is a "celebration" of bygone years when life was not on a "time-clock". This aspect is readily visible as guests chat and rock on wrap-around verandas on 2 levels. A rich dark wood treatment highlights bar and dining area which usually overflow with patrons. Exciting special monthly EVENTS are the inn's specialty and are well attended. Programs include Wine Celebrations, Mystery Week-Ends, Antique Car Races and others. Deskclerk usually greet visitors but at times this is done by a corps of friendly "inn kitties" ! GIBSON INN has a first class reputation in southeast states----I suggest reservations ! ! !

Apalachicola Fl   Gibson Inn Market St & Ave C
Open Daily   904-653-2191

COOMBS HOUSE INN 1905

Reception room of this Victorian Manse was created to "dazzzzle" ! Entry is dominated by black cedar walls, beamed ceiling, tiger oak flooring and handcarved oak staircase, tiger oak flooring and handcarved oak staircase. A silky golden blonde (Sandy) greets most guests . . . . Friendly dog is everyone's "teacher's pet". Leaded glass windows blend with far east carpets, Chinese urns and ornate appointments. Coombs 3 story mansion is crowned by a widow's walk has 10 guest rooms 9 fireplaces and period furniture. Choice colors "waterfall" from drapery bedding and upholstery. The inn's owner who is a national award winning interior decorator did all the meticulous restorations of each room----Home is within the HISTORIC DISTRICT ! ! ! A stone-throw away are additional quarters in Coombs Cottage Annex.

Apalachicola Fl Historic Bed & Breakfast #80 at 6th St
Open Year Round 904-653-9199

TROPICAL ISLANDS

ST GEORGE ISLAND

Length is 14 miles. Over 50% of island is a STATE PARK ! ! ! West half is hundreds of "skyhomes" of (every design known to man) which overlook Gulf beaches. It is an unstable island due to width (widest part is 1-1/2 miles) . . . . SGI has fine beaches. Wild storms occasionally rake the shores which become steeper in Winter due to heavy waves which move sand to offshore bars. *New* BIKE PATH (1 Mi) was on "overflow" with skaters & peddlers. SGI's 30 miles of sugar-sand gulf and bayfronts make it a VACATION R-E-N-T-A-L MECCA. If you prefer an "escape hatch" without a high-energy profile "dis is da place" ! ! ! Each March St George "spices" up its pace a bit . . . . It is home to the largest regional CHILI COOK-OFF in the U.S of A.!

Apalachicola Fl (6 Mi East) South On SGI Bridge
Open Daily C of C 904-653-9419 Bike Rents
SGI State Park 904-927-2111

FLORIDA RIVER ISLAND

A 5,000 acre WILDERNESS with amazing natural diversity. Island is a "part-timer" hemmed in by Apalachicola and Florida rivers and floods only during high water. Most of year conditions are *hi-n-dry.* Sturdy hardwoods of hickory, green ash, sweetgum and sugarberry are everywhere. Some to 100 feet! We were delighted with the new 1997 *bridge and rock road construction* leading to heavy timber stands shoelaced with old logging trails. Some roads groomed, others are not. Beaver, deer, marsh rabbits are often sighted while food hunting. Breeding birds (99 kinds) live in or visit the island. Late Spring can bring hundreds of gliding Swallow-Tailed and Mississippi Kites soaring overhead. Creeks and lakes dot the interior. CANOERS use a good ramp next to the bridge giving access to Florida River. Near by on a "rise" are grassy well manicured camping sites (self-contained). Day picnic tables overlook the languid stream. Florida River Island's remoteness and isolation appeal to backwoods hikers and bikers. Also access for horseback riders. Pack plenty of grub, water and a compass. Map Pg 54

Apalachicola Nat'l Forest   Rd 65 to Rd 379 West On Forest Rd 188 (.5 Mi)
Open Fri-Noon to Mon-Noon
N.W.F. Water Management 904-539-5999

600 POUND DEER & RED WOLVES

The 9 by 4 mile island is a gem in Florida's coastal necklace. Isle is a 12,358 acre wildlife refuge. Sambar deer (America Elk Cousin), Zebra, elands and other exotics were imported to ST VINCENT ISLAND in 1948. Sambar thrived. They number about (75) in 1997. Breeding program for (bashful) Red Wolves is recent and "dicey". There is mom, dad and a "pup" ! Franciscan friars setting up missions in 1625 named the island. In 1868 George Hatch, mayor of Cincinnati, Ohio bought St Vincent for $3,000. His grave is marked by small white cypress fence and stones near (West Pass Channel). In 1908 a Dr Pierce made improvements to the island. He built cottages, barns, dams, sluice-gates and 30 MILES OF ROADS----I tramped (10) of them! A 9 mile stretch of sun-splashed shores is a sight and gift from heaven. St Vincent was purchased in 1968 by Nature Conservancy for $2.2 million ! ! ! Easiest access to refuge is from Indian Pass where about 1,000 ft separate mainland and island. Boats and lots of w-a-t-e-r b-i-k-e-r-s scoot across the narrow channel to dockhouse area where trails begin. ANNUAL FALL TOUR provides boat & island tram transportation ! ! ! Map Pg 56

Apalachicola Fl   Rd 30 At Indian Pass Boat Ramp
Boat Access Only
Open Daily Daylight Hours   St Vincent N.W.R. 904-653-8808

THE CAPE

It was----a cape----now it's an island. A ship channel was dug in 1954 which lopped off the cape from St George Island. Ship channel is called SIKES CUT . . . . remember the "He-Coon", Sikes??? Island goes by (3) names . . . . The Cape, Little St George or St George State Reserve. The 10 mile *boomerang shaped isle* absorbs shock-waves from gulf storms. 1960's military operations squashed some dunes but other relic ridges topped by sea oats and scrub are visible. Interior consists of ponds, marsh, pinewoods, willow swamps and savannahs. Some trees still exhibit "cat-faced" scars from turpentine operations. Bayside at GOVERNMENT DOCK are old camp buildings from this business. Swimming and sunning is a "joy" on cape's *remote beaches* ! ! ! Primitive C-A-M-P-I-N-G is allowed at West Pass, Sikes Cut and and Govt. Dock. Hiking is on old logging roads, beaches and overwash areas. An 1852 LIGHTHOUSE still bravely faced seaward in 1997 but its lean increases with each storm! Reserve is open year-round for recreation. Map Pg 57

Apalachicola Fl South on Apalachicola Bay
Open Daily BOAT ACCESS ONLY
Cape St George State Reserve
S.G.I. State Park Info 904-670-2111
Adventures In Paradise 904-653-8463
Jeanni's Journeys 904-927-3259

LIGHTHOUSES AND FORTS

A STORMY CAPE – A TIPPY LIGHTHOUSE

Landspit juts into the Gulf and has had a "bad rep" since 1766. Frightful events began when the ship, TIGER, sank on a ledge marooning crew and passengers on the cape. Due to starvation and cannibalism after 81 days only 1 man and a woman survived. They were rescued by British soldiers. Three beacons were erected on CAPE ST GEORGE. One in 1883, a second in 1847 and a third in 1852. Towers 1 and 2 got chucked into the sea. Lighthouse 3 is "teetering" at an alarming angle ! ! ! If a local effort ($$$$$) to save the lighthouse is successful the following is what you would see on a visit----A 72 ft high tower on brick pilings. Wall thickness at base is 4 ft. Top is 2 ft. An interior *circular iron staircase* passes 6 reinforced windows stopping 6 ft shy of the historic lantern. As of late (1996) 4,000 sand bags, many wooden beams and crews of workers have propped up this historic sentinel. Wouldn't it be a WONDER if the 145 year old structure extended its life into the 21st "century"???? Map Pg 57

Apalachicola Fl   Across The Bay On Little St George Island
Boat Access Only

A MOVE IT OR LOSE IT LIGHTHOUSE

Like a feline with 9 "lives" this shore tower has been rebuilt 6 times since 1838. Hurricanes or shifting sand kept dunking the beacons until a steel skeleton structure was built in 1885. By 1919 when its steel "tootsies" were in standing water the skeleton was disassembled and put on high ground where it stands today. In the light (not used today) is a rare 1859 third order French-made lens which still bears chips made by Confederate musket fire! I found the morning light good for photos. Because of GPS (Global Positioning System) CAPE SAN BLAS LIGHTHOUSE "light" was turned off on January 18, 1996 after 111 year of steady service. The tower and keeper's dwellings may not be entered. There are access points for "admiring"! Military gate is sometimes open. If not, a short 1/2 mile walk is possible. Another approach is via the beach.

Cape San Blas Fl   Cape San Blas Lighthouse
Open Daily   (Exterior Observation)

THE NEGRO FORT

First built by British in 1814, it was a base to recruit Blacks and Indians in War of 1812. At war's end the British left the fort including artillery, munitions and 700 kegs of gunpowder to a group of Free Blacks, Indians & escaped slaves. The post was known as THE NEGRO FORT and attracted settlers who farmed and traded on the river. In 1816 four American sailors went ashore for water supply and were killed by blacks and indians. American military retribution was swift. The Negro Commandant and the Indian Chief refused to surrender even though 300 people had taken shelter in the fort, most being women and children. Gunboats began a short lived attack with their 5th shot being a "hot shot" red-hot cannonball). It hit the powder magazine and the fort completely disappeared---- The explosion was heard in Pensacola (100 miles west). The dead numbered 270. After 1818 Andrew Jackson named the site FORT GADSDEN using it as a base to pursue Seminole Indians. Last use of the fort was by Confederate troops in 1863. I walked the 78 acres seeing berms outlining the old fort. Steamboats during the exporting "cotton era" once docked here and on grounds is a huge boiler from one of them. It is the IRWINTON which caught fire and sunk in 1838. An outdoor *Interpretive Center* has six informative exhibits with many artifacts. CEMETERY is nearby. Facilities include picnic shelters and restrooms.

Sumatra Fl (5 Mi South) Off Rd 65 Take Forest Rd 129 (Dirt)
Open Daily 8-Sunset
Ft Gadsden State Historic Site 904-670-8988

CROOKED RIVER LIGHTHOUSE 1894

No "chubby" men every applied for keeper-duty at this sentinel. Bottom entry door looks to be only 17 inches wide on the 115 foot tower. Structure is steel with 4 outer support legs and many cross beams. On the lintel over the doorway is a large metal star and two-thirds way to top is a window . . . . Lighthouse straddles a 30 foot mound and peers over 3 or 4 acres of lovely short needle pines. As is the tradition for all lighthouses, this one has its own SIGNATURE (paint-job). Top half is red-rust & bottom is white. Below the glass light are 2 (one below the other) circular walk-around outside balconies----bet views are superb----but climbing up is not allowed. You can get some excellent pictures from selected spots on the mound. Lighthouse is about 100 feet north of Hwy 98. MOST DIFFICULT TO SPOT BECAUSE OF TALL TREES. Lighthouse cost $40,000. It has a visibility of 10 miles out in the Gulf ! ! !

Carrabelle Fl Hwy 98 (Northside) 2 Entrance Roads (1 Sand & 1 Paved) Lighthouse is .4 of a mile west of Carrabelle Beach
Open Daily Outside Viewing & Photos

MUSEUMS

LARGEST ESTUARINE RESERVE IN AMERICA

An estuary is where salt & fresh water meet and mix. Apalachicola NATIONAL Reserve covers 194,000 acres of land, water and islands . . . . Each day 16 billion gallons of fresh river water flow into the bay. About 500 folks a month visit the museum which has exhibits and displays explaining the estuary system. I was impressed by an extensive SHELL COLLECTION including spindles, Giant Tun, Tulips (7 inches), shark eye, lightning whelk, rare spotted junonia, clench's helmet, angelwings and on and on! A skull display had black bear, alligator, bull shark (1-1/2 ft). A spiney lobster shell was 2-1/2 ft. Other display show Indian Trade Pipes, Spear Points Pottery Fragments and Replicas. A "kid favorite" is a WHALE BACKBONE found on nearby St. George Island State Park----*Lab Room* is all touch & use----preserve jars contain octopus, sea robin and lots more. An annex contains several tanks. One had 4 species of turtle. (The Suwannee Cooter) was a mite too friendly. Gliding in the fish tank were sheep head, mackerel, angelfish, spotted sea trout and 10 more types . . . . Blowfish looked right "mean"! *Living Honey-Bee Hive is a popular exhibit.*

Apalachicola, Fl   Market St. (North End) Go East .2 Mi.
Apalachicola National Estuarine Research Reserve
Open Mon. Through Fri.   904-653-8063

APALACHICOLA MARITIME MUSEUM

A 2-part museum . . . . Indoor section is small. Significant exhibits include historic binnacle (case for ship's compass), an original oil lamp off GOVERNOR STONE 1877, a weighty wood double block & tackle, old-time lifting equipment, 1870 drill press and a solid brass "hand" bilge-pump! Hanging on the walls are lots of artifacts used during the period of steamboats and regal sailing vessels. Two vintage motors are a 1925 Johnson and the old Palmer "workhorse"! Display cases contain other memorabilia and some neat photos----2 additional exhibits were a mite "tubby" to squeeze into the museum----They are the 41 ft. SEA DREAM and 35 ft. VENEZELLUS ! ! ! These are 2 historic fishing boats owned & maintained by the *museum.* You may admire them both. SEA DREAM is on *Water St.* & VENEZELLUS is on *Market St.* To enjoy 2nd part of Maritime Museum, read on . . . .

"CRUISE" THE MUSEUM
1877 GOVERNOR STONE

Your chance of a lifetime is a 2-hour cruise on the South's *oldest operating sailing vessel*. Daily trips on the restored 63 ft gaff-rigged schooner are a delight. Gov. Stone carries a great press of sail.

Built for shallow waters it was used for U.S. Merchant Marine training, "rum-running", freighting and oyster buying boat. On your gulf sail-away you may even hoist the 1400 square feet sails (sometimes takes 2) or take the helm or let "Cap & Crew" do the muscle stuff while you enjoy! S-U-N-S-E-T C-R-U-I-S-E-S are a "favorite" ! ! !

Apalachicola, Fl - Market St. Daily Trips
Apalachicola Maritime Museum 904-653-8708

"COOL IT"

And he did "just that". Dr. John Gorrie worked to bring down fevers (106 degrees) of Yellow Fever patients. He devised an ICE MACHINE to cool sick rooms. At GORRIES MUSEUM you'll see a replica of the 1851 machine with which the doctor unknowingly laid foundations for *air conditioning and refrigeration*. 1830 to 1860 was the "cotton era" when Apalachicola city and river had many lavish plantations. The museum has fine exhibits of this period . . . . A bale of cotton was 4 x 4 x 5 ft and weighed 500 lbs. One display is a 5 ft 1850's schooner's wheel that you *operate* to see a 15 ft plantation diorama move before you ! ! ! Visitor's are surprised on seeing NATURAL BROWN COTTON----so soft! Dr. Gorrie never made "a penny" from his invention but he received the highest honor when his statue was place in Statuary Hall in our U.S. CAPITOL in Washington, D.C. There is plenty to hold interest in this small museum.

Apalachicola Fl Corner Ave D & 6th St
Open Thur thru Mon 9-5 Not Thanksgiving, Christmas & New Year's
John Gorrie State Museum 904-653-9347

ST VINCENT VISITOR'S CENTER

The center is an example of good things in small packages. It encapsules the island's plant and wildlife. You will see an antler (12 inches) of a whitetail deer (130 lbs). For comparison you view an antler (27 inches) of a SAMBAR DEER (745 lbs) which was introduced to the island in 1908 and has thrived ! ! ! I admired a beautifully preserved specimen of the Red Wolf (6 ft nose to tail). Once plentiful in the southeast they are now extinct. On the island is a Red Wolf breeding program. One of several dioramas depict oyster catchers snowy egrets feeding in the many marshes on St Vincent. Be sure to trek "upstairs" for other exhibits. One is a *7 foot topographical map* showing dunes elevations and deep trenches at east & west pass. Kids enjoy the interactive button pushing displays. I found the walk-around outside porches of visitor center super for photos and filming.

Apalachicola Fl   Market St (North End) Go Right 2nd Floor
Open Mon-Fri 8-4:30   904-653-8808

NATURE PRESERVES

LIVING IN THE FAST LANE OR NEW "ISLAND" HOME

St George Bridge & Causeway total 4.3 miles. One causeway (.5 Mi) is home to the largest *breeding colony* of LEAST TERNS on Florida's Gulf Coast. They nest on both sides of a busy road. April through August their numbers can rise to 600 pair ! ! ! They dart swoop and glide among vehicles . . . . but not without risk . . . . I saw 2 victims. Everyone is interested in the 10 inch black-capped flyers. In Spring college students erect 35 MPH signs and several state agencies have built up a 23 acre "NEW ISLAND" in Apalachicola Bay. It consists of sandy dredge material and goes by the awful name of DISPOSAL AREA 2.1----birds don't care! Over time it is hoped the terns will abandoned their wreckless nursery habits to breed on ISLAND 2.1. It can be seen from high point of Apalachicola bridge . . . . I piloted my small boat, Lil' Dipper, out to (2.1) where hundreds of terns, water-skimmers Franklin Gulls and other shorebirds were raising a territorial hullabaloo. When visiting causeway use S-L-O-W speed and do not approach "nesting areas".

Eastpoint Fl   (April-August) Off Hwy 98 South On St Geo Island Bridge
Open Daily   St George Island Causeway Bird Sanctuary

WILDERNESS PRESERVE & DUNE RIDGES

You need 4 pieces of equipment to enter these extraordinary 1,650 acres----2 sturdy legs & 2 strong feet ! ! ! Five miles of hiking reveal major *high stabilized dunes*, foredunes, ancient beach ridges, blowouts and other barrier island geo-features. Freshwater marshes were a surprise. *Autumn* brings great numbers of migrating birds . . . . 209 winged flyer types have been sited (210) if you count MONARCH BUTTERFLYS who winter in Mexico! There are 3 hike routes: one is a shell-sand road cutting through peninsula's interior, 2nd follows St Joe Bay, 3rd hugs the gulf front. Carrying capacity for preserve is 25 persons per day or one group of 40. Primitive camping, swimming, fishing are allowed----there are no facilities----PACK IT IN, PACK IT OUT . . . . Map Pg 59

St Joseph Peninsula State Park *Wild Preserve West of Cape San Blas Rd 30-E*

Open Daily NEED PERMIT 904-227-1327

OLD STEAMBOAT LANDINGS

ERA OF STERN-SIDE & PADDLEWHEELERS

By 1844 Apalachicola River had 26 "landings" along its 106 miles. COTTON was the crowned king of cargo. Some steamboats went to 140 ft boasting lavish passenger quarters and dining salons. Between boiler explosions and river *snags* the life expectancy of a steamboat was 7 years. Scores of them rest on the river bottom. Loading wharfs were on the "mighty" Apalachicola while others located on side streams like the Chipola River, Owl Creek etc. I visited (V-I-A C-A-R) 18 landings. Some were easy access, others are more remote . . . . Exploring them was fun. Each landing has its own character and present-day use. Below are several you may enjoy ! ! ! Map Pg 62

HOWARD CREEK

Pleasant driving on Doc Whitfield Rd (PAVED) 8.6 miles because canals hem both sides of road and were brim-ful of 6 inch *white hyacinths* (thousands) blooming in August. A short span over Indian Bayou indicates low wetlands having extensive cypress & willow growth. A .3 mile dirt path ends at the landing which flows into nearby BROTHERS RIVER. About 75 trucks toting boat trailers parked every-which-away and 50 "vintage" campers huddle near the ramp area. You know the village is a sportsmen enclave by HOWARD CREEK COUNTRY MART. They sell crickets and what a ruckus they make ! ! ! Locals are quick with a "howdy". You may wish to visit on a WEDNESDAY. This is *community lunch day*----For a modest donation you eat yummy fare and meet folks. It happens at 11:30 at the Firehouse. Side streets have names of animals or fish. Many more permanent homes have year round residents.

White City Fl North on Rd 71 East on Rd 387 (Doc Whitfield Rd) 8.6 Miles
Open Daily Howard Creek Country Mart 904-827-8055

BRYANT LANDING

After much study and talking with local folks, I believe the words LANDING and LODGE both refer to old steamboat dockings. Bryant was my *favorite* of the 3 landings in the area. Gorgeous hardwoods line the short (paved) road to CHIPOLA RIVER. A most t-i-d-y "mini village" of cabins and neat mobiles are shadowed under tall maples and sycamore. Landing is very wide where I viewed 4 (most tidy) homebuilt houseboats. Still water mirrored 2000 year old Cypress on opposite bank. Chipola is a river of unusual GEO-FEATURES and lush wild beauty! You'll see *caves, limestone bluffs and shoals*. One is called "LOOK AND TREMBLE FALLS" (below SR 274 bridge) ! ! ! ! !

Bryant's Landing Rd 381 A (East) Open Daily Boat Ramp

DOUGLAS LANDING

There are 2 roads leading in. Don't take the first. It is dirt. Second road is paved. Terrain is more upland but can change quickly to low bottom. Several brick homes and riverfront campgrounds comprise the landing.

Douglas Landing Rd 381 A Open Daily Boat Ramp & Camping

WILLIS LODGE

A 4 mile drive (paved) beside cornfields and cow pastures ends at a *well manicured upscale campground* near Brothers River. Some lovely rigs parked here. Nearby was a high-water mark for July 1994 flood of 17.6 ft. Not far up river at GASKIN'S STILL they boast a (high-water??????) mark of 22.1 ft ! ! !

Willis Lodge SR 381 A Open Daily Boat Ramp & Camping

COTTON LANDING

In 1836 there were 20 STEAMBOATS operating on Apalachicola River. Almost 60,000 bales of cotton were exported that year. Farmers brought their bales to docks like Cotton Landing on Kennedy Creek where pole boats, bateaux or steamboats would take the cotton down to Apalachicola for export. There is still a north Florida town called COTTONDALE from that long ago era . . . . The landing on Kennedy Creek is still there but ever so "hushed". It's a pretty spot in green woods with a boat ramp and small camp area. Fishing is said to be "real fine" in the creek. More to my taste are the plump blackberry bushes that bloom each Spring. Lower Apalachicola River Basin also has the largest stand of TUPELO OR OGEECHEE TREES in the world. They bloom in April and May and their honey has an unequaled "rep" for clarity, purity and sweetness----Cotton Landing is a neat spot to picnic. High water mark for great flood of July 1994 reads 20.5 feet ! ! !

Sumatra Fl *Rd 379 (N.W. 3.2 Mi) Forest Rd 123 (West 2.8 Mi)*
Take Rd 123 B (West .7 Mi)
Open Daily *Primitive Camping*
Apalachicola Nat'l Forest 904-926-3561

THE RIVER STYX

This day's exploring led to surprise and amazement as I hunted up an old steamboat dock, WHITE OAK LANDING. At 2.4 miles you cross 2 one-lane wooden bridges where woods enter a River Swamp Hydrick Phase. White Oaks blanket the area ranging 60-120 feet with diameters of 2-3 feet. Leaves can be 9 inches and half as wide. Deer & hog relish the acorn . . . . Landing is on a curve of the River Styx where grassy plots alternate with campsites. All are PRIMITIVE. Stately White Oaks spread a green canopy. There is a good ramp for boat launching. A short distance before the landing exists the most curious looking WOODS CAMP I've ever seen. Assortment of about 100 shelters defying description. Combinations of lean-to's, yurts, and hunt cabins. Looking at a multitude of leaning walls, rolling floors and wobbly underpinnings I was astonished at the number of folk living in these architectural gems! I found this group of fishers and hunters to be a friendly bunch ! ! ! A solid dirt road between the camp and White Oak Landing turns to the south. It is a special trail to HIKE BIKE OR DRIVE as it is shoe-laced with l-u-s-h woods, flowers and wildlife. I followed it for 2 miles hoping it would go over the river so I could brag, "I crossed The RIVER STYX and *made it back"* ! ! ! Map Pg 62

Apalachicola Nat'l Forest *Off Rd 379 (Paved) West On Rd 115 (Dirt) 3.3 Miles*

Open Daily

PARKS WITH PIZZAZZ

LAFAYETTE PARK 1832

Often trees are removed to make a walkpath. Here, a red brick pathway was created to *detour around the trees*. Park's focus is its LIVE OAK TREES. Most being 100 to 300 years old. Notice the arching branches which were used in ships as ribs & keels. During War of 1812 "Old Ironsides" built of Live Oak had cannonballs bounce off with no penetration. I ceased counting trees at 105 . . . . you finish! Park perches on a high bluff overlooking bay and distant pass. At park center is 100 ft circular brick promenade with an octagonal 8 columned gazebo big enough for the Marine Band. Ringing the park are several showcase VICTORIAN HOMES! Period lamp posts, picnic tables, grills & playground round out facilities----Folks love the $1,000,000 dollar view and enjoy brown bagging breakfast or lunch at Lafayette----almost "dis-remembered", the 600 foot STROLLING & FISH PIER (great sun-sets & moon rises) ! ! !

Apalachicola Fl *Ave B & 14 St* *Open Daily*

PICNICS BESIDE I.C.W.

This lovely park overlooks Florida's INTRACOASTAL WATERWAY. Lunching on the bank of a wide canal is an adventure because *many craft* daily utilize this water "Highway". I saw two 400 ft barges being joggled east by the "little tug that could"! Tables have shelters and grills. Facilities include kiddy playground, basketball court and restrooms. Under the *65 ft high bridge* (marvy view from top) both banks hold their quota of avid fisher folk. North side of bridge it is possible to nudge your car near canal and watch all the ACTION. A few boats are usually moored at the small dock & ramps area.

White City Fl   White City Park Northwest Side of Bridge on Pridgeon Rd
Open Daily   904-827-2900

CHAPMAN BOTANICAL GARDENS

Even the parking lot was "dandied-up" with tall 7 ft feather grass plants. Entrance is through a high pergola laced with vines. Period black lamps topped by white globes line the walk. Green open spaces give a sweeping grandness to the promenade which is dotted with streamers of Weeping Willow. Decorative iron benches allow for leisurely study of park plantings which include hollyhocks on west fence red, pink and purple crepe myrtle and perfumy oleander. Kids love the old-timey drinking fountains with "foot pedals"! A BOARDWALK under dignified Cypress passes over a swampy area. You'll feel a temperature drop and a coolness wash over you here. Overhead birds were pounding out rhythms while down below a shiny turtle munched weeds. A gazebo is focus of a lovely circular patio----All this on about 8 acres ! ! ! Garden is in memory of Alvin Wentworth Chapman 1809-1899. He was an internationally known botanist and resident of Apalachicola. He read Greek, Latin and French. Learned German at age 80 . . . . As in our modern age his life was not without strife. He married Mary Ann Hancock in 1839. During 1860's (CIVIL WAR ERA) the couple separated over the issue until war's end. He was a "union man", she a Secessionist. ! ! !

Apalachicola Fl   N. Market St   Open Daily

APALACHICOLA RIVER WAYSIDE PARK

This small green oasis has perched beside the mighty Apalach since 1967. Actual name is Gaskin Wayside Park. Further down river is a hamlet called GASKINS STILL! Could this be same gent'??? No matter, spot is lovely restful park for day picnics. Short scenic (2.3 Mi) drive winds beside Chipola River Cut-Off. Tall groves of swamp bottom hardwoods line the road. I walked the long bridge over Dead Lakes for superior photos of this natural "PHENOMENA"---You see submerged cut Cypress stumps big enough to drive a car through and thousands of ancient Cypress (every shape & size) ! ! ! Road ends at park which has 10 sheltered tables, some grills & bathroooms. I enjoyed watching craft jouncing around sandbars for best fish holes. There is a good ramp if you've a boat to dump. Do amble about a clean (4 Street) community adjacent to Gaskin Park!

Wewahitchka Fl   Rd 71 (Downtown) East on Rd 22 (Lake Grove Rd) 2.3 Mi

Open Daily

RESTORED HISTORIC DISTRICTS

40 BLOCKS OF RESTORATION
National Historic District

Since 1993 the "rash" of historic home renovations has been as plentiful as chiggers on blackberry bushes! A wonderful "TOSSED SALAD" of classic styles spans 1830 to 1900's----plenty of *ante-bellum* "pin-ups" too! For some eye-poppers on your walking or windshield tour start at Ave B and C. Here are Queen Anne style which was America's dream home from 1876 to 1896 ! ! ! The Q.A. home is ruled by asymmetry . . . . gables, towers, wings, verandahs and balconies poke out in all directions. I walked or rode my bike on north-south streets (4th to 17th) and found many architecturally significant homes and even some modest ones dripping with bric-a-brac & gingerbread. I counted WINDOWS . . . . many ornate homes had 40 ! ! ! Really old towns have a-l-l-e-y-s. Apalachicola's run (north & south). Alleys kept trash pick-up and wagon deliveries to the back yards. Also if your mate came home "tippy", neighbors couldn't see . . . . Bet they could. Remember the 40 windows! On corner Ave D & 5th St is a Steamboat Style (1846) 2 story home. Within the historic district are several old churches and old Sisters of Mercy Convent (2 story brick, circa 1900). Renewal fever has spread north of Hwy 98 (Ave E) and while *not* the BON-TON area of town many lovely restorations have been completed. If home owners are in their yard stop-n-chat. You'll find em' friendly and "bustin-button" proud of their town. See Historic Home Identification Page. See Map Pg 49

Apalachicola Fl   C Of C 904-653-9419

COMMERCIAL & MARITIME HISTORIC DISTRICT

My roving began on the waterfront next to 3 story 1938 Courthouse on WATER STREET. Of the 40 brick cotton warehouses built in 1836 only *2 still stand*. Road was called "Street of Granite Fronts" because of granite facade columns and lintels over doors. Streets are broad . . . . they needed to handle wagons & animals pulling huge loads. Shrimp fleet *docks daily* to off load catches sold to large seafood distributors. 1884 Grady building stands newly restored. It was once a hardware and ship chandlery for steamboats and full square rigged vessels of 3 masts. Ambling north you may browse 1909 Wefing's Marine Store or Apalachicola Times having 8 foot thick flooring as it once housed a generator plant! *Scores of "darling shops"* on COMMERCE STREET and the "cross" avenues deserve exploring . . . . Unusual gifts. Try THE SUNFLOWER. Like goodies??? Doors don't stop swinging on DOLORES' SWEET SHOPPE. Historic SPONGE EXCHANGE warehouse attests to the town's G-r-e-e-k presence. 1938 Oasis Bar was a bank before depression era . . . . Notice small octagonal floor tiles. Old Greek grocery and Economy Cash Stores are "leaners" awaiting restoration----they make great photo shots! MARKET STREET is unique with its (4 step curbs), 1907 Gibson Inn and shopping ANNEX. Always busy is 1905 SODA FOUNTAIN (28 flavors). Both sides of Market are lined with yesteryear's brick & wood business houses still catering to shoppers these many years later. Lots of c-h-o-i-c-e-s for restaurants. If you've time and want a chuckle watch the "action" at CONFUSION CORNERS (Market St & Ave E) This intersection has 3 stop signs, one go street and a central blinker light. Only the "locals" know (when-to-go). Out of towners see-saw, hesitate, creep up, slam brakes and execute other original drive maneuvers at this corner ! ! !

Apalachicola Fl   Water St., Commerce St & Market St

RIVER TOWNS

WHITE CITY

I'd call it more of a hamlet----about 700 strong----Modest homes line the canalside town where many people are employed in logging and fishing. I was told that no black people ever lived in White

City . . . . hence, its "moniker"! Residents gained national attention in 1992 by voting in the *youngest elected official in the U.S.A.* He was 18 year old county commissioner, Michael Hammond . . . . must of done a pretty fair job 'cause he ran again in 1996 at ripe age of 22! Another claim to fame for the town. It has hosted since 1982 a well-known annual BASS TOURNAMENT with 1st prize of $4,000. Held each September. Do visit (N.W. side of bridge) HAMMONDS COUNTRY STORE. I found it interesting and folks friendly. One wall holds 125 old brass combination post office boxes. Store sells 16 mouth-watering kinds of ICE CREAM . . . . they even have chocolate ! ! !

White City Fl Hwy 71 North of Bridge Open Daily

POLLY PARROT HISTORIC SITES & TYRENE'S

It's all in BLOUNTSTOWN (pop. 2500). Town's past is interlaced with Apalachicola-Muskogee-Creek Indians and named for Seminole Chief Blount. The 1st (bi-lingual) marker in Florida was erected In front of historic 1904 brick Calhoun County Courthouse which is a *restored "beauty".* Marker is written in *English & C-R-E-E-K INDIAN*. One paragraph speaks of Polly Parrot who dug in her "moccasins", refused to go west to new lands and led followers in 1823 to a wilderness just north of Blountstown. I ambled main street (Hwy 20). Here are a few blocks of *historic storefronts* housing varied businesses. Rd 20 leads to one of the state's most historic bridges (1.7 miles). Its steel girders and arches span the ever-flooding APALACHICOLA RIVER. Over the years a flashing lead car has been on 24 hour duty to guide wide-load vehicles across the narrow bridge! Toodle down River Street (S.E. corner of *new* courthouse) to Neal's Landing where in late 1800's steamboats docked to load cotton for European ports. Blountstown is a "charmer" and so is TYRENE----She is a "Southern Magnolia" with the business acumen of a "Wall Street Tycoon" ! ! ! If it's 'tween 8 a.m. and 5 p.m. park your wheels at 311 N. Main St at "Tyrene's". Inside you'll find 4 bustling businesses . . . A florist shop, gift shop, wedding boutique and an *eating emporium* that "tops the charts"! The cafe caters to "tummys". Menu lists 12 kinds of sandwiches, umpty-ump salads, full meals, steaming home-cooked soups and a bakery case that no one can resist. Tyrene's business savvy prompted faxing weekly menu to 75 local businesses, also new is

Frequent Diner Card. Newest enticement is CUSTOMER "WHIMS"----On file are your favorites served with precision & promptness . . . . Just south of restaurant is a small railroad monument park with restored historic M & B RAILCARS on display!!

Blountstown Fl   Hwy 20   Open Daily   C of C 904-674-4519

SOPCHOPPY
"YOU'VE COME A LONG WAY BABY"

Town of 600 souls was known as WORM "FIDDLING" CAPITAL of Florida. Families passed down the occupational technique of----grunting worms for fishermen. An old cut leaf truck spring is staked in the dirt. It is twanged and vibrations send the "crawlies" dancing to the topsoil . . . . Kind of a (dirty) trick . . . . You come to DANCE and end up on a HOOK! H-m-m-m, lots of marriages start that way ! ! ! 1997 finds Sopchoppy a part of the Eco-Tourism scene. Canoers love the spiral course of the l-o-n-g stream flowing through mid-town. Bluffs to 15 ft are common. Small downtown is renovating. I ambled by a double 1912 brick business, a couple of old store fronts with classic indented windows and double doors. Old feed store is a crafts boutique. On Railroad Ave patiently waiting its preservation is the wooden depot. Tiny post office still uses yesteryears brass lockboxes. Next door is AUNT MARTHY'S BOARDING HOUSE slated for fix-up as a private home----if it doesn't fall down first! Scores of old homes (not fancy) but historic & in good repair are tucked back on Yellow Jacket St, Camillia Ave, Rose St and Summer St. Still in use is the old riverrock schoolhouse. Tour out on Rd 375 to Greenough Rd and Mt Beeser Terrain, Canopy Lane and Mount Besser bridge are charming. West on Rd 22 I checked out what locals call THE ROAD THAT GOES TO NO WHERE . . . . and it does!

Sopchoppy   Off Hwy 98   North on Rd 319

TOWN IN A TIME CAPSULE

Not a *single traffic light* is found in APALACHICOLA or the whole of Franklin County ! ! ! Residents number 2,759 and most speak with the soft "drawl of the South". Since 1821 till now all facets of daily life center around the bay and 106 mile Apalachicola River. During steamboat era (1820's) to Civil War it was a world famed cotton port. Men built grandiose homes, churches and businesses----THE HISTORIC DISTRICTS (residential & commercial) overflow with 200 such structures within a 2.5 square mile area. Renovations are stunning. Best spot to view shrimp boats and anything that "floats" is from the "T" pier *under the bridge* next to Hendel Park Ballfield (Water St). Dolphin frolic in this narrow channel to gulf & bay. Bring lawn chairs . . . . set-a-spell . . . . action at the dock is like watching the movies! Apalach is a family place so I felt comfortable strolling at night. Some evenings town is lit up like a markee. Don't get stressed out over *missing street name signs*, ya can't get lost . . . . Apalachicola will always remain in a cocoon because of geography (bay & rivers) and the fact that over 50% of Franklin County land is owned by state and federal governments. Unusual sites and sights turn up on every Apalach corner. One such is SHADOW LANE or SHADY LANE (they gave 2 names to 1 street). Why Not ! ! ! Anyhow, it is lovely. Just like APALACHICOLA TOWN ! ! ! Map Pg 49

Apalachicola Fl   C of C 904-653-9419

SCENIC DRIVES

YENT BAYOU SHORE DRIVE – 10 MILES

Ride begins at "home of the tongers" which is Eastpoint where generations of families have harvested OYSTERS. On south side of Hwy 98 bobbing at anchor are shallow draft oyster boats. Long handled tongs (rakes) are used to gather the succulent shellfish. Countless wholesale & retail stores line the waterfront----yes, I bought shrimp, crab and oysters and yes, they were exceptional tablefare----For next 6 miles your buggy is *never over 30 feet from glistening "sound" waters*. Two distant islands are always in view, St George and Dog Island. Near Emerald Point your ride is more elevated (12 ft) and white island beaches are visible. Near drive's end is some unusual and lovely geography. Signs indicate (short) YENT BAYOU BRIDGE. To the north are heavy woods and saltwater lagoons. *To the south* at Hidden Beach sign is one of the Gulf's highest dune middens (40 ft)! ! ! View from top is exhilarating. Good shell sand roads curve about 1,000 ft back to one of most pristine beaches in the panhandle! Plenty of Cedar near the lagoons. I retraced the scenic drive and found several small pull offs (south side Hwy 98) just big enough for a picnic. Gentle slopes allowed wading in "sound" waters where shelling was surprisingly rewarding . . . . this was near PORTER'S BAR CREEK BRIDGE.

Eastpoint, Fl   To Yent Bayou Hwy 98 Go East

INDIAN PASS AND BEACH DRIVING

About 20 miles of Hwy 30–A hug the north bank of St Vincent Sound. Green pinewoods and occasional oak hammock are the "backdrop". Several short shell roads (southside) open up to vistas of calm sound waters and nearby St Vincent Island! Near mile 17 go south on Rd 30-C. At this juncture is early 1900's wooden INDIAN PASS TRADING POST which serves steaming gumbo, fresh bay oysters and other choice seafare! Opening time is f-l-u-i-d ! Rd 30-C passes over Indian Lagoon and small bridge where canepolers fish . . . . Next 3 miles (paved) are behind *primary dunes* on a narrow peninsula. Hunchback trees top sandy ridges where sit family beach homes . . . . At drive's end is action-packed Indian Pass . . . . Folks are launching boats or personal watercraft, beach lounging & lunching, surf fishing or shelling. Spot is popular because it's a short distance (900 ft ??) across West Pass to gleaming white beaches of St Vincent Island whose 14 miles are wilderness and uninhabited ! ! ! Good place to "photo". BEACH DRIVING ALLOWED WITH P-E-R-M-I-T obtained at Franklin Co. Courthouse in Apalachicola. Good beach access is back on Rd 30-A near Sweetwater Shores----bring grub and needs. There are no facilities.

Apalachicola Fl   West on Rd 30-A   Directions Above   Open Daily

CREEKS & BAYOUS BYWAY

Tour start is at Green Point (Hwy 98). Go north on Rd 65. First bridge spans CASHIE CREEK. Still lagoons mirror tree islands surrounded by tidal waters where crab-pots sometimes bob . . . . Lovely Vistas! August brings lanky pink marshmallow blooms. Next bridge crosses WHISKEY GEORGE CREEK ! ! ! Don't ask . . . . In spite of moniker the area is serene and pretty with a small boat ramp on S.E. side. Looked like wonderful *Canoeing*. I found pull-offs for shady lunching . . . . bring a blanket as no tables . . . . great views, though. Several dirt roads lead into *Tate's Hell Swamp* of 67,882 acres. Some roads passable, some not. Number 3 stream is DOYLE CREEK. Also has small ramp and would make for an intriguing "float". Under bridge 4 flows DEEP CREEK. Upstream appears tropical and mysterious. On S.W. corner is neat picnic spot (no facilities). Primitive Camping is allowed at the 4 Creek sites. Extending your drive north lands you in Sumatra (weensy hamlet) named for type of wrapper tobacco grown hereabouts. Continuing northwest on Rd 379 puts you on the national forest APALACHEE SAVANNAHS SCENIC BYWAY which flows through wet lowlands, rolling uplands, Magnolia & Cypress stands and grass Savannahs that are one of the richest botanical areas in the U.S. ! ! !

Apalachicola Fl (10 Miles East) On Hwy 98 North on Rd 65 to Rd 379
Open Daily Spring & Summer (Best Seasons)
USDA Forest Service Bristol, Fl 904-643-2282

SEAFOOD "A LA" APALACHICOLA

MEET & EAT THE ROYAL FAMILY

Since 70% of Apalachicola residents make a living from the fishing industry they are justly proud of their royal trio. King Oyster, Queen Shrimp and Prince Crab reside in (3) aquatic preserves between the mainland and several barrier islands. Passion for oysters began with the Romans and has steamrolled down through the centuries. Apalachicola Bay provides 90% of Florida's and 10% of the national oyster harvest ! ! ! Some facts : : : : Spat are free floating infant oysters. Local barges periodically blow scallop shells onto submerged preserves so spat can attach and mature. In 1-1/2 to 2 years they are harvestable. Bivalves are vegetarian flourishing only where fresh and salt water mix. When feeding they'll filter 25 gallons of water in 24 hours. Tongers (oystermen) off-load their skiffs on bay docks where they are cleaned in rotating cages and whisked to local and distant kitchens. Of Florida's top 20 types of seafood harvested, #2 spot is held by SHRIMP. All day all night "Apalach" shrimp fleet about (100) boats put to sea searching for the succulent crustaceans. Some facts : : : : There are (4) kinds; pink, white, red and brown. Critters have 5 pair of legs. First 3 for walking. Shrimp spawn offshore in deep water (early Spring to early Fall). Young-uns float into estuaries to mature. Shrimp are sold by "count per pound". Range is 10 or less per lb. (large) to 300-500 (smallest)! Regional shrimp make sumptuous tablefare.

BLUE CRAB holds #3 spot in Florida seafood production. Some Facts : : : : They are omnivorous. Female claw tips are bright red (as in human species). They enter semi-hibernation in Winter . . . . They are "yummy" to eat ! ! !

SOUTH'S BEST SEAFOOD EATING

QUESTION . . . . How can a tiny town of 2,700 support 22 local restaurants??? ANSWER . . . . Visitors come from many southern states to enjoy the "gourmet fare" of Apalachicola kitchens. BOSS OYSTER (waterfront landmark) serves oysters (15) ways----tee shirts read "Shut Up & Shuck" ! ! ! At CAROLINE'S (same grounds) one does not eat, one d-i-n-e-s! Their signature seafood presentations are chef secrets. GIBSON INN kitchen creates delights of shrimp & scallops dijon within their historic 1907 Inn. I think (all) Apalach businesses have "Zero Tolerance" for brown bagging lunch----At 11 a.m. sharp they make calls to (all) eat spots for daily "lunch specials". This leaves 45 mins for decision! I figure Apalach is America's only town with a (2 hour) lunch tradition ! ! ! During my stay I developed this ritual----"When In Rome" . . . . In 30 days I sampled perhaps 14 restaurants. Following are some menu "tempters" : : : : steamy gumbo, bisques, chowders, shrimp in fresh tomato bloody-mary sauce, fluffy oyster omelets, COLD RAW OYSTERS ON THE HALF SHELL, sauteed dill grouper, shrimp, oyster & crab burgers, hot butter-dipped crab claws, seafood alfredo splashed in White Wine, and Death-By-Homemade bread & biscuits . . . . After 30 days of this I departed Apalach not for lack of money but for lack of "gastronomic will-power ! ! !

Apalachicola Fl   Choice of (22) Restaurants

SEAFOOD-2-GO MARKET DISTRICTS

To "buy" or not-to-"buy" ? This is NOT the question . . . . but how MUCH ! ! There are 2 (2 mile) retail, wholesale fish house areas. They both are dedicated to the maritime fishing industry and enjoy special protection of Franklin County Land Use "Regs". Most companies front on the bay for off-loading cleaning and packing. I bought most of my purchases at a place called SEAFOOD-2-GO which was so squeaky clean, it had no fish smells. Owners (Dottie & Tracy) are typical folks in the business. Industrious, family focused and going the extra mile to please customers. Some shops are 4th generation owners. Iced down counters of "rolly-polly" shrimp, tangy oysters, lively blue crab and other seafare make buying decisions weighty ones. About (45) fish houses dot the water front----their "credo". The seafood on your table *"today"* slept in the bay "last night" ! ! ! Be sure and tote extra coolers when visiting this maritime community. I loaded up for a 9 hour drive home. On arrival my seafood treasures were fresh as morning dew ! ! !

Apalachicola Fl *West District on Hwy 98, West of 26 Ave----*
East District on Hwy 98 East of Gorrie Bridge at Eastpoint Near Tonger Skiffs Breakwater
Open Daily

SOMEPLACE DIFFERENT

SCIPIO CREEK SHRIMP FLEET

About 100 boats tie up at this deep "back-water". Day or night captains are busy fixing gear, loading supplies or mending nets. Fishing is often a FAMILY AFFAIR with mom and "wee folks" assisting or accompanying dad on trips. *White boots* are a trade-mark and the men are proud of their heritage . . . . Some fishing families go back 5 generations. I strolled the basin asking lots of basic (girl) questions. In-shore bay boats are usually under 38 ft. Off-shore craft are 72-90 ft staying out 10-14 days. Best LOOK & PHOTO spots are (2)----Oyster Hill (north of basin) and 2nd floor (north porch) of St Vincent N.W.R. building (S.E. basin corner)----Scipio fleet harvests many kinds of fin and shell fish but S-H-R-I-M-P is #1 with Apalachicola Bay (alone) producing 20% of this succulent table fare ! ! ! ! Boat "names" will make you smile. I liked Little Dipper, Southern Lady, Nixie, Buddy's Boys. Scipio Creek is home to *Florida BIGGEST commercial fishing fleet*----ya gotta' visit----

Apalachicola Fl *Market St North (Dead-End)* *Open Daily*

OLD ST JOSEPH CEMETERY 1835

During mid 1800's Yellow Fever Epidemic worked havoc on Florida's population. This small historic cemetery contains mass burial sites of Yellow Fever victims who lie in "unmarked" graves.

There is scroll listing of people who are believed to be buried here . . . . It reads like a WHO'S WHO *of pioneer families* from scores of Florida counties ! ! ! Several raised brick monuments resemble "above ground" plots in famed New Orleans Cemetery. One marker is in memory of Captain Kupfer who died at sea aboard the schooner, Herald on 9,19,1840. He was 36. A brick path winds about markers and under blooming trees . . . . I did not use the pretty rest GAZEBO . . . . I like to keep "moving" in a cemetery ! ! !

St Joe, Fl   On Rd 384 (Garrison Ave) at Cemetery Rd   Open Daily

A CHOICE PLACE

Your choices are: GULF SWIMMING, A SCENIC DRIVE, PICNICS, HIKING, FISHING, BIKING, BOATING or PHOTOGRAPHY ! ! ! S.G.I. State Park has 1,962 acres where visitors do their own thing. I managed 5 of activities above! A 4.4 mile (paved) road runs beside sandy beach and low dunes topped by Sea Oats. Dunes that did not get "crewcuts" by Opal in 1996 are 15-20 ft high. A shell road will soon add 3 miles to (east end) of *Scenic Drive*. There are 10 pull-off overlooks where you may also swim or surf fish----catches are flounder, sea trout, whiting & Spanish Macks. Gulfside are 2 picnic areas with humongous shelters plus all amenities for day in "el sol". Island geo-features are shallow coves, long sloughs, salt marshes, Oak & Pine woods. Also on BAYSIDE are 2 small islets (Goose & Marsh Islands). A 2.5 mile trail runs from campsite to Gap Point. You may see *"cat-faced"* slash pines from turpentine operations of a by-gone era. CRABBING is popular on sound side. Here is a boat ramp & short dock. State park is 8 miles long directly on the Gulf of Mexico. I saw many bikers who cycled 4.5 miles to road's end . . . . Here is stunningly beautiful 30 foot "SUGAR HILL . . . . I guarantee your camera will come out of the case! Map Pg 57

St George Island, Fl   Off Hwy 98 South on SGI Bridge
Open Daily 8-Sunset   SGI State Park 904-927-2111   Camping

"OLE" 10 FOOT HOLE AT CITY MARINA

That's what some local youngsters used to call this deep water anchorage. It seems to be the town *gathering spot* and a more PICTURESQUE place you'll not find . . . . It peeks out over Apalachicola Bay (mostly 10 ft deep itself)! To the south (5 miles) its' easy to see 2 large islands. Snugged up at the basin's edge are 40 or 50 boats. Some classics, some "Huck Finn" craft. About 6 rivers plus 'WHISKEY GEORGE CREEK" plow into the bay so it is common to see boats dockside from Georgia, Alabama or Louisiana. Jewel in this setting is 900 ft. wide PIER PROMENADE ----"stuff" is always happening here. I visited twice a day and felt like a "local" when even the pooches gave me friendly "licks". Pier's end has large shelter with benches and W-O-W do they catch fish out there ! ! ! Rest gazebo (2) pretty up the basin's north shore. In and out boat ramps at marina are top flight. You have room and facility for 6 craft to launch at a time . . . . if they're not zig-zag trailer backer-uppers (like me).

Apalachicola Fl   Bay Ave At Bridge

APALACHICOLA ANCHORS – THE STORY

About 6 feet high and close to 500 lbs. They lie all over the town. In back yards, front yards, parks, by roadways and in storefronts . . . . This is where they came from . . . . Back in early 1900's Apalachicola was a major center for export of Cypress lumber to Europe. Ships needed deep anchorage (15 ft or more). Hook would be set at Little Sand Island near St George Island in West Pass where barges could ferry the lumber to and fro. In any kind of blustery weather the anchor would "bury up" and a pull out was impossible. Captains would bouy the anchor so other ships might tie to it also laying their anchor. Sure enough----another "blow" would make-up and another anchor was lost. Thus, a repeating cycle of Use-It & Lose-It continued until 1950 when shrimping boats began using TICKLER CHAINS. These drag on bottom-mud and cause shrimp to jump into the nets. Early years of tickler chain use resulted in much wrecked equipment ruined by *"snagging".* As shrimpers, motors and ticklers became bigger and more powerful the snagged anchors were raised and bought ashore. *About 75 were toted to town*. In 1958 the owner of WEFING MARINE on Water Street bought one of the sunken "hooks" for $10. It now lays outside the historic brick marine store lending an air of dignity and charm---- Without even trying, I located 17 old anchors around town----How many can you find ? ? ?

Apalachicola Fl

CATCHING ARGOPECTEN IRRADIANS CONCENTRICUS

Or "Bay Scallops"! My first experience with chasing these small "jitterbugs" was in 1986 in Pine Island Sound near Ft. Myers . . . . This was a rare appearance for scallops to that area . . . . Not so in *St Joe & Apalachicola Bays* in north Florida FAMILIES PLAN VACATIONS to coincide with the Scallop Season (JULY & AUGUST). Scallops hide in shallow water having heavy concentrations of seagrass----Wearing a light beach shoe you can feel the tip of the shell---Now for the tricky part. I wear a light glove for the "grab" as the little guys are surprisingly quick! They can move 10 or 12 inches up or down or sideways by clapping their shells, then webble-wobbling through the water. Actually they're an easy catch! Of the 53 Aquatic Preserves in Florida St Joe Bay is the ultimate for SCALLOPING. *You don't need a boat*. I've found treasure troves of the luscious shellfish near BLACK'S ISLAND in St Joe Bay. APALACHICOLA BAY & ALLIGATOR HARBOR can also be good harvesting sites. 1996 restrictions were 2 gallons (unshucked) per person. *Tread easy on seagrass*, it's the Scallops Home ! ! ! Have fun, I did.

Apalachicola Fl *Apalachicola Bay or St Joseph Peninsula State Park on St Joe Bay or Port St Joe Hwy 98*
Apalachicola Nat'l Esturine Reserve 904-653-8063
Adventures In Paradise Boat Tours 904-653-8463

CHESTNUT HILL CEMETERY 1832

My interest in cemeteries began when my mom gave me driving lessons in one! This burial ground is under sturdy Chestnut, Oak, Cedar and fat Pine trees. Grounds boundaries are black iron fencing . . . . What is *most unusual* are 35 or 40 family plots each fenced with individual highly stylized black iron work. The scrolls, arches, curves, curlycues, and pickett work required skilled craftsman. H.F. SIMMONS PLOT FENCE is 1 example. O-r-n-a-t-e and massive stones are a history book of colorful founders and molders of north Florida's past. Interred here are ship captains, yellow fever victims, gallant Confederate Soldiers who served at Gettysburg and world renowned botanist, Dr. Chapman. You'll notice inscriptions denoting a strong German presence in early Apalachicola. Earliest BORN-DATE I found was Eliza King (1797)

Wow ! ! ! Some locals say this hillside graveyard was originally an Indian midden----Before leaving, stroll to west fence boundary to view 3 stout 90 ft PINES which look just like OAKS ? ? ? I'll bet this is some of that fancy "splicing" attributed to the famed botanist, Dr. Chapman ? ? ?

Apalachicola Fl Hwy 98 (Ave E) Between 6th & 8th Streets
Open Daily

RIVER "KING", APALACHICOLA – 106 MILES

It is Florida's longest being used commercially since 1820. Most cargo was cotton shipped to Europe via sailing schooners, "Aristocrats of The High Seas". Steamboats carried cotton bales from up river landings to Apalachicola wharves for loading on schooners. By 1844 there were 28 daily dockings by steamers. 1828 to 1928 saw 205 stern and side wheelers plying the waterway . . . . Today the mighty "APALACH" still plays a vital role in our states commerce, by way of seafood harvesting and recreation. For 30 days in my boat, Lil' Dipper, I discovered the river's diversity. The mix is one of tropical hardwood islands, umpteen river systems and a maze of backwater creeks & bays. Even with charts, locations were "fuzzy", but, I was never lost----FOR TOO LONG---- ! ! ! South of mid-river I passed THE RIVER STYX (I didn't cross)! Near Wewahitchka extensive SAND BARS build up. Great for lunching and cool-downs! I met all type of craft including families of jet skiers from 30 miles up river! Near Bristol (north) are BLUFFS rising to 195 feet with magnificent stands of forest atop them. Luxury yachts from Atlanta often journey down connecting river systems all the way to Apalachicola on the gulf ! ! ! If you use your boat get MAPS at Welfings marine 252 Water St. Below are some TOUR BOAT businesses.

Apalachicola Fl Apalachicola Belle 904-653-8803
Governor Stone 904-653-8708
Adventures In Paradise 904-653-8463
Jeannie's Journeys 904-927-3259
Boss Guide FISHING 904-653-8055

MOONRISE SUNSET PIER

A breathtaking S-I-M-U-L-T-A-N-E-O-U-S moonrise-sunset occurs 3 to 4 times a month----Be there----Stroll to end of City Pier just south of Battery Park. Near 8:15 p.m. (summer) a silver dollar moon lumbers up over St George Sound to the east while to the west a blazing gold sun sinks softly in waters of St Vincent Sound. Watching this phenomena is becoming a tradition in APALACHICOLA ! ! ! The pier's bay location gives open views of moon creeping behind St George Island and shimmering moon-beams across bay waters. Glance west to see royal reds & purples thrown off a fiery sun which silhouettes marsh hammocks and tree islands. I admired gliding water skimmers, tiny bait fish dancing atop the waves and 3 tubby manatee feeding in tall grasses near the dock. Far out the pass in the gulf shrimp boat's twinkling lights were visible. This moon-sun co-event lasts perhaps 20 minutes but the MEMORY *will be with you a "lifetime"* ! ! !

Apalachicola Fl   City Pier Bay Ave & 6th St
Open Daily   Check Calendar for Moon Phase

FORT COOMBS ARMORY 1901

Construction is brick painted white. Its 2 stories are dotted with many arched slit windows. An exterior tower buttresses the south-east corner. Armory is home to the FRANKLIN GUARDS whose volunteer militia units date back to Seminole Wars of 1830's. Inside arched portal is a CIVIL WAR SIGNAL CANNON used to alert Confederate soldiers of a yankee advance towards town. Interior treatment is a surprise. Done in dark highly polished Cypress and Pine. A double wood staircase displays decorative spindles. Sliding Cypress track entry doors look super and still work and are closed for hurricanes. Unusual ceiling is supported by many 50 ft (one-plank) beams. Ceiling is wood also sloping to a gentle curve on sides. A balcony lines north and south walls. Theater type seat-ing in (3 tiers) gives fine viewing of events below in massive hall. North annex room boasts a mammoth fireplace & mantel of river rock . . . . color is a (shocker) though ! ! Room is "loaded" with exhibits, flags, memorabilia and photos of Franklin Guards partici-pation in past conflicts. This includes a flag and sword from 1898 Spanish American War. On display is a TONTINE AGREEMENT signed by veterans of W.W. II. When only 3 of them are living they will toast their comrades with a bottle of Cognac which is locked in the (Armory Safe). In 1997 there were 18 of these men left. Fort Coombs Armory is what I call a "Living Museum" because it is used for community events, even the high school prom ! ! Forty men and women still drill and train here. Ft Coombs is one of 2 armories (owned by the state). The other is in Key West.

Apalachicola Fl   Corner of 4th St & D Ave
Open Mon-Fri 9-3

RAINBOW ON A RIVER

I perched atop this "rainbow" for 30 days and nights. Recalling tales of a "pot-of-gold" at rainbow's end I found RAINBOW INN itself to be the treasure. All guest quarters sport *outdoor balconies overlooking the busy Apalachicola River*. I've attended parties where there's never-a-dull-moment, but a steady 30 days ? ? ? I tried not to-miss-a-thing! Inn has scores of docks and boat slips. Some captains dock their craft with style, other "landings" can become quite hilarious. Motor & sail luxury yachts from west and southern states make daily visits as "Apalach" is a major stopover on the INTER COASTAL WATERWAY. Best views for "goings-on" is an outdoor-indoor 2nd level deck of The Rainbow. Here you may sip, sit or quip amidst glorious nature & water scenes. I loved the constant (24 hour) parade of shrimp boats plying the nearby channel. Nor did I skip the *nightly sailing* of 1877 GOVERNOR STONE, a 63 foot 2 mast gaff-rigged schooner. It departs Rainbow's dock each evening for sunset cruises, dolphin watching and moonlight sails ! ! ! Rainbow security is handled by Miss Patches (guard-kitty) . . . . don't let dozing posture fool you, she has 17 years experience! Guest's most serious problem is the d-e-s-i-r-e to "eat" all day. Aromas float up to balconies from BOSS OYSTER, a seafood waterfront eatery where seats are never vacant! For fine dining try CAROLINES On The River. All rooms face east overlooking America's largest estuary system----and beyond----is the wonder of *A Sunrise Over The Rainbow* ! ! !

Apalachicola Fl   Rainbow Inn & Marina 123   Water St
Open Daily   904-653-8139

TWISTY RED OAK RIVER FUN

Creek and Seminole Indians named this river and CAMPED here . . . . You can too ! ! ! Indian words for twisty and red oak were hard for pioneers to say. They renamed the river SOPCHOPPY . . . . an "improvement" ? ? ? Campsites are in CITY PARK beside the river. Acreage is well manicured. Lots of grass, attractive river rock circling trees and most inviting settee swings beside a shell riverwalk. Red Oaks umbrella the park and picnic shelters (plenty) both for family and large groups. Public boat ramp and float dock are on Sopchoppy which is a *lovely canoeing stream* both north & south ! ! ! This small park is *one of the prettiest* I've seen in ages. Come to DAY PICNIC. Campsites (10-15) have electricity water and bathrooms. Town holds concerts and events regularly.

Sopchoppy Fl City Park Open Daily
904-962-4611 904-962-3873

APALACHICOLA ANNUAL FESTIVALS & EVENTS

FLORIDA'S OLDEST SEAFOOD FEST

Since 1963 – Nov – 1st Weekend – 3 Days – Est. Attend 20,000

City's in high gear as guests come to scarf back World's best oysters. Competitions include oyster shucking & eating with winners gulping a minimum of (240) in 15 mins ! ! ! Seafare booths serve crab, shrimp, oysters and fish in a variety of recipes . . . . plenty spicey gumbos too. Art & craft exhibits are top-o'-the-line. Parade has a (what else) maritime theme. BLESSING OF FLEET (very large) is a fest highlight. Yes, more . . . . Fireworks, King Retsyo (Oyster) Ball, Demonstrations: Tonging–Castnet Throw–Shucking, constant "center stage" entertainment. Headliners i.e. MARSHALL TUCKER BAND in 1996! Come "let loose" at Florida's largest & original MARITIME HAPPENING.

Apalachicola Fl Battery Park & All Over Town
C of C 904-653-9419

HISTORIC TOUR OF APALACHICOLA HOMES

Since 1992 – May – 1st Sat.

Tour includes 12 to 24 historic and architecturally noteworthy structures. Town boasts over 200 of these. Tour sponsored by

Trinity Episcopal Church 1838. A knowledgeable host greets visitors at each site. For a nominal fee you'll have a million dollar experience!

Apalachicola Fl   Trinity Episcopal Church 904-653-9550
C of C 904-653-9419

GIBSON INN ANTIQUE CAR ROAD RACE

Since 1986 – Mid April

24 classic "gran-dames" chug their way from Panama City to Apalachicola. On arrival at Gibson Inn (1907) cars and drivers are bedecked in finest array----period clothing and glitzy autos take center stage.

Apalachicola Fl   Gibson Inn 904-653-2191

LARGEST CHILI COOK-OFF

Since 1983 – March – 1st Sat – Est. Attend 5,000

50 Cooks compete. Winner goes to National Cook-Offs. Giddiness presides at this "rite of Spring" on a famous 29 mile barrier island.

St George Island Fl   904-927-2396

ST VINCENT ISLAND N.W.R. TRAM TOUR

Since 1990 – October – 1st Week – 5 Hour Tour

Boat & Tram transportation provided for tour of 9 mile "primitive" island. Home of 600 pound Sambar deer, white tail deer, boar 'gator and much birdlife. Only marked grave is that of George Hatch who once owned the island and died there . . . . gorgeous beachfront . . . . 10 types of habitat!

St Vincent Island NWR   904-653-8808

HISTORIC HOMES GUIDE

APALACHICOLA
RESIDENTIAL HISTORIC DISTRICT
&
MARITIME COMMERCIAL DISTRICT

Walking Or Windshield Tour

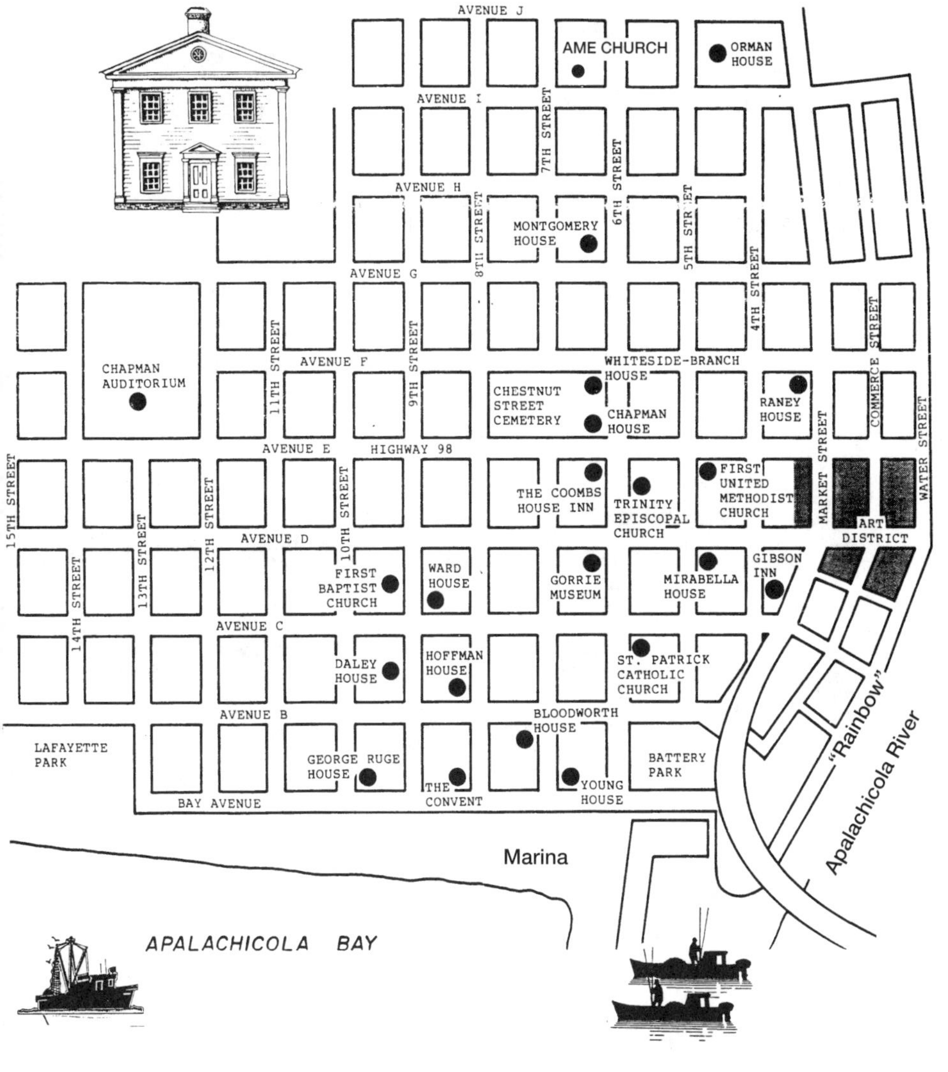

HISTORIC HOMES

Style Guide

Greek Revival 1815-1840

Features

- Columns & Capitals
- Greek Temple Effect
- Six Over Six Window Panes

Gothic Revival 1835-1880

Features

- Pointed Gables
- Finials at Peaks
- Diamond Shape Panes
- Medieval Motifs

Carpenter Gothic 1870-1910

Features

- Wood Deco on Peaks
- Ornate Railing Designs
- Carpenter "Whims" on Posts & Cornice
- Often Called "Gingerbread"

Queen Anne 1875-1900

Features

- Mix of Shapes & Textures
- Non Symmetrical
- Porch Fine Spindlework
- Brick Chimneys Fluted

HISTORIC HOMES

Style Guide

Stick Style 1875-1900

Features

- Exaggerated Sense of Structural Support
- Siding Vertical Shingles or Horizontal
- Eave Brackets

Southern Plantation 1800-1900

Features

- 2 Story Verandah
- Tudor Chimneys
- Basic Farmhouse Style with Design Adjustment for Climate

Bungalow 1900-1930

Features

- Clapboard Wood Frame
- Main Roof Over Porch
- "Elephantine" Porch Posts
- Chimney & Foundation is Usually Fieldstone

Colonial Revival 1885-Present

Features

- Heavy Boxy Style
- Hipped or Gabled Roof
- Palladian Triple Windows
- Doorways with Fanlights & Slender Sidelights

HISTORIC HOMES

Style Guide

Vernacular Italianate 1865-1885

Features

- Projecting Bay Windows
- Rood has Massive Cornice & Brackets
- Ornate Window Frames
- Door & Window Tops Often Rounded

Early Georgian 1720-1760

Features

- High Foundations
- Door Light Transom
- Roman Classicism Design
- Pitched Roof

Late Georgian 1760-1780

Features

- Classical Details
- Lavish Entrance
- Semi-Circular Fanlight over Ornate Door
- Columns & Pilasters

Federal 1780-1820

Features

- Post Revolution
- Elliptical Fanlights over Doorway
- Simple Window Frames

Queen Anne Tower House

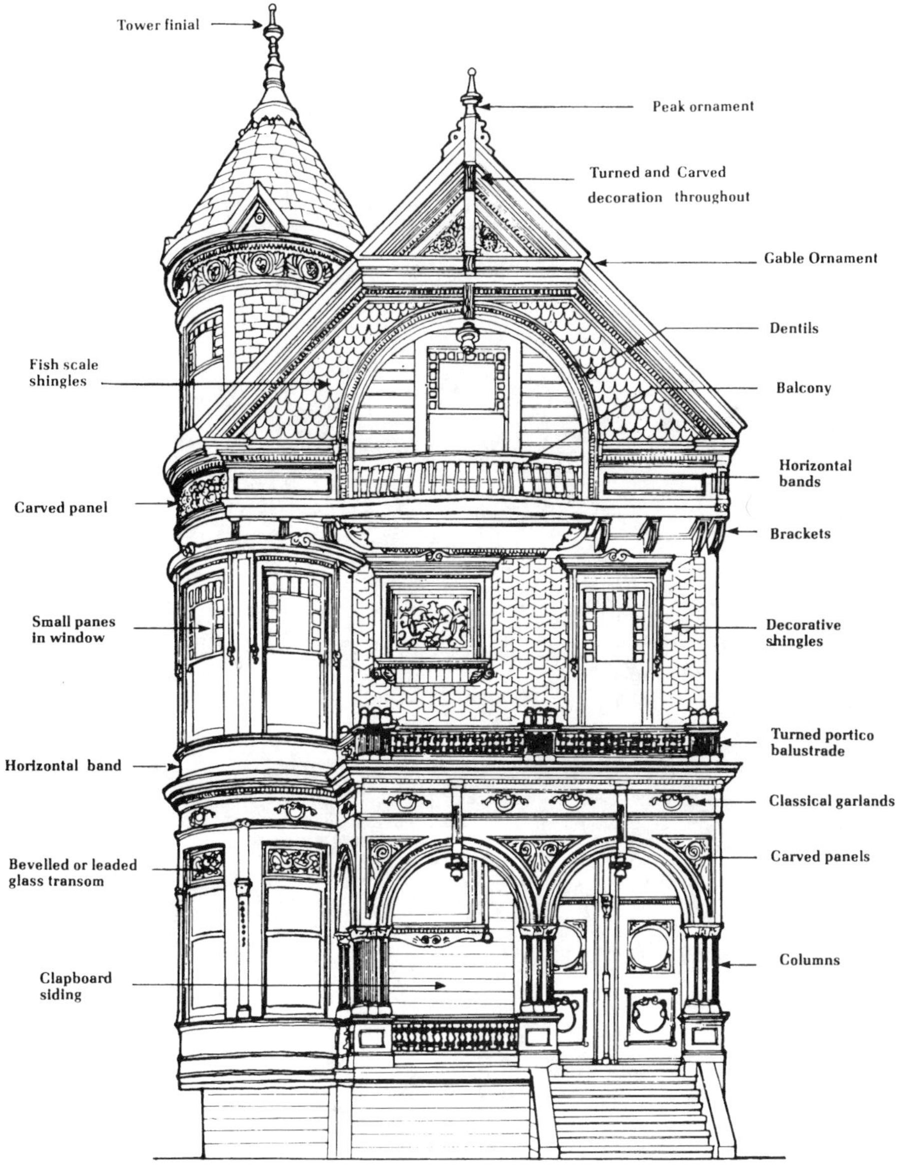

Architectural Detail Terms

FLORIDA RIVER ISLAND

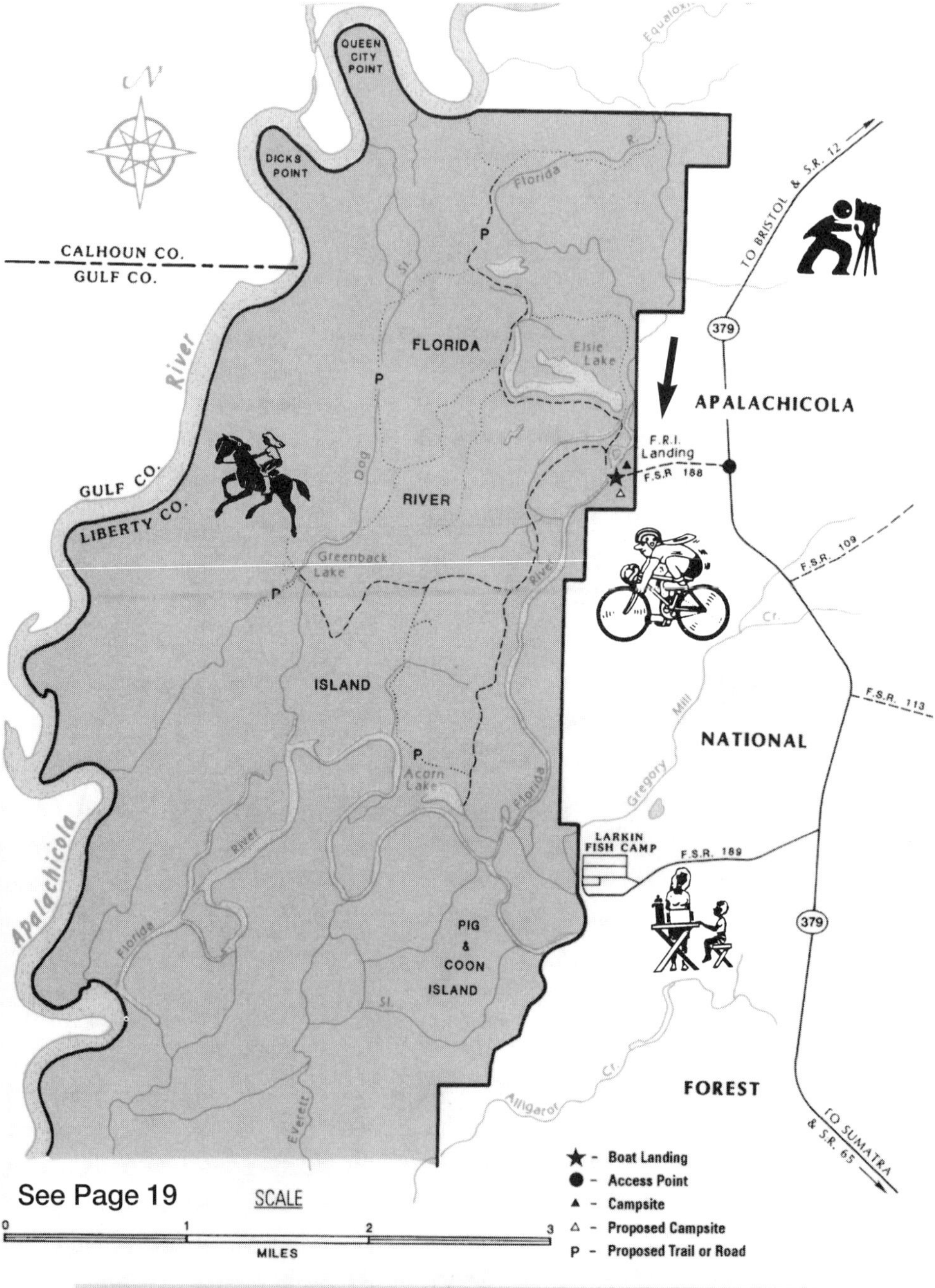

See Page 19

APALACHICOLA RIVER BASIN
Boating & Canoeing

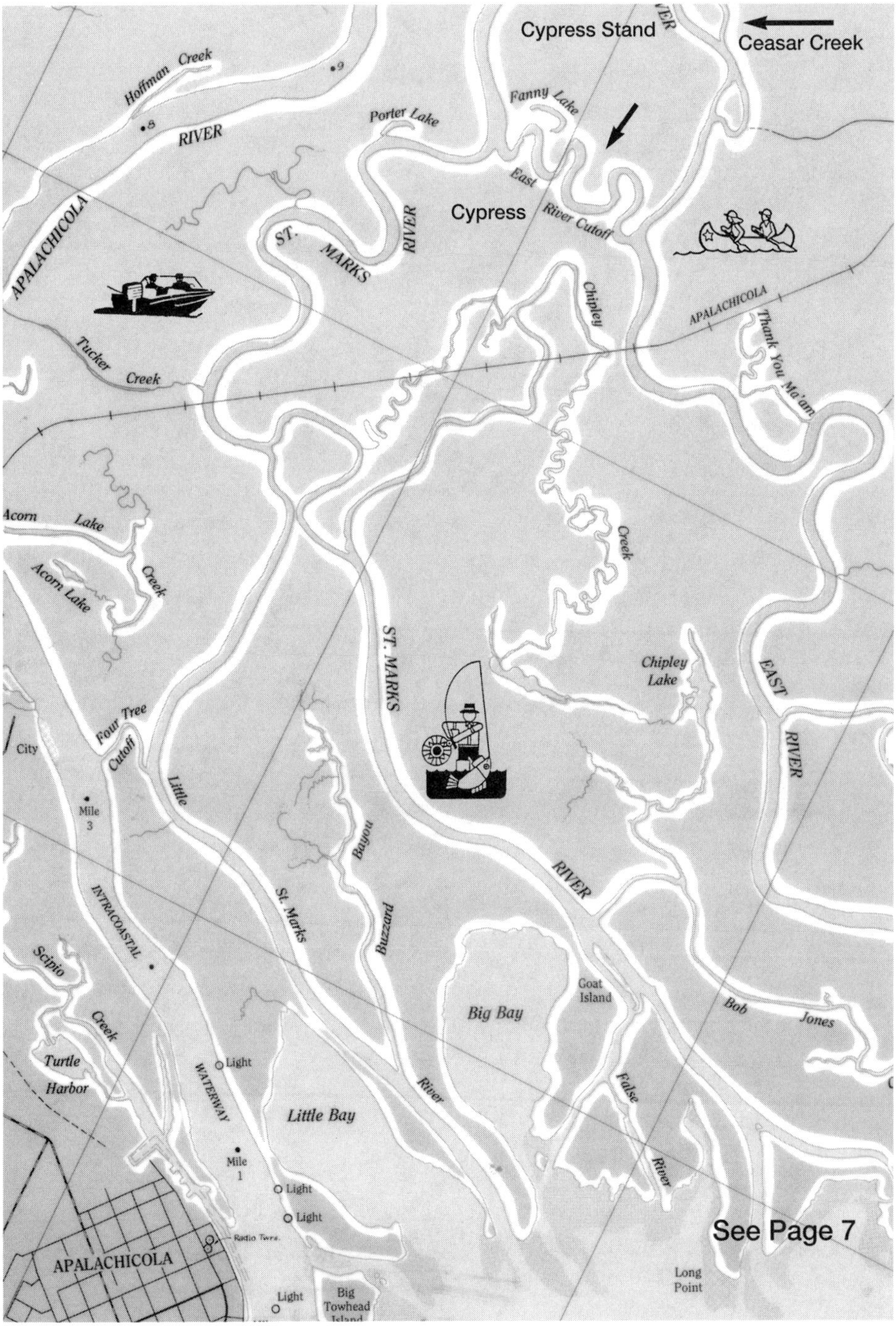

St. Vincent National Wildlife Refuge

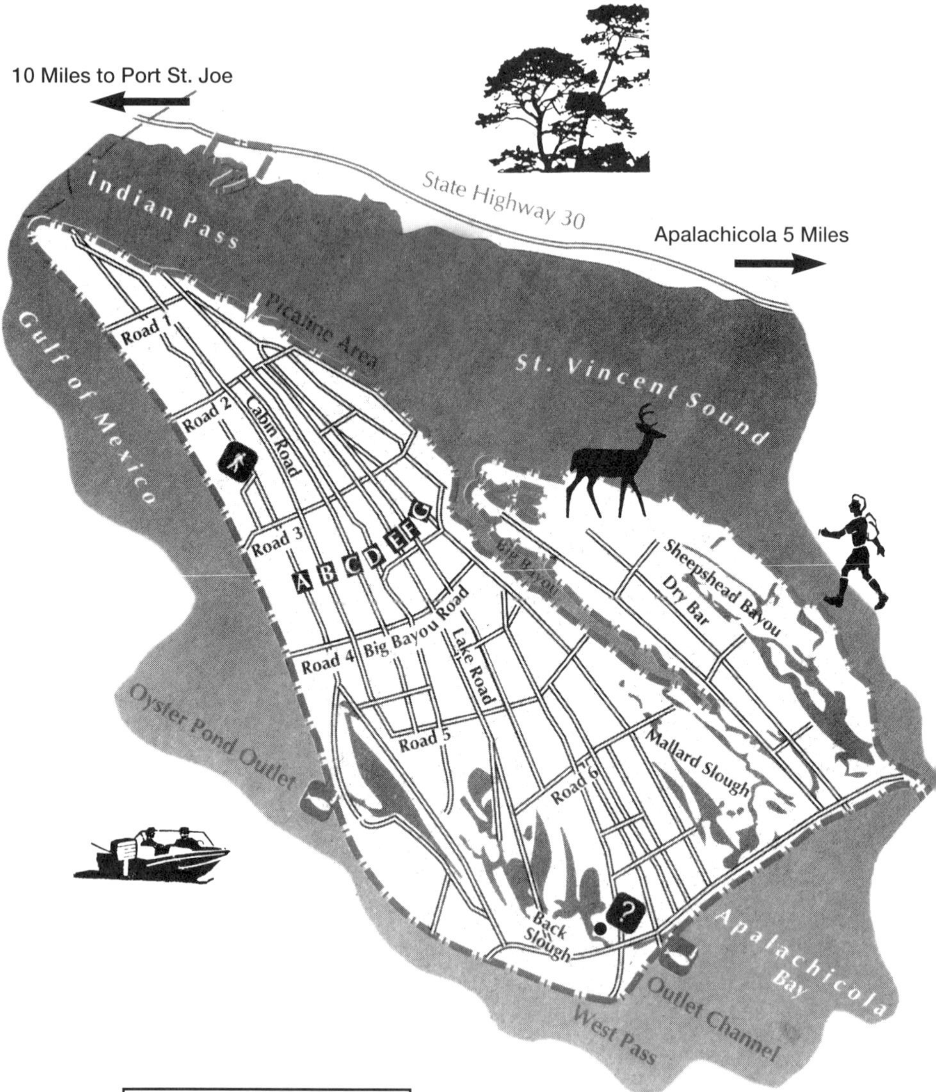

- G. Hatch Grave
- 14 Mile Beach
- 80 Miles of Roads
- 12,358 Acres

See Page 14

ST. GEORGE ISLAND STATE PARK

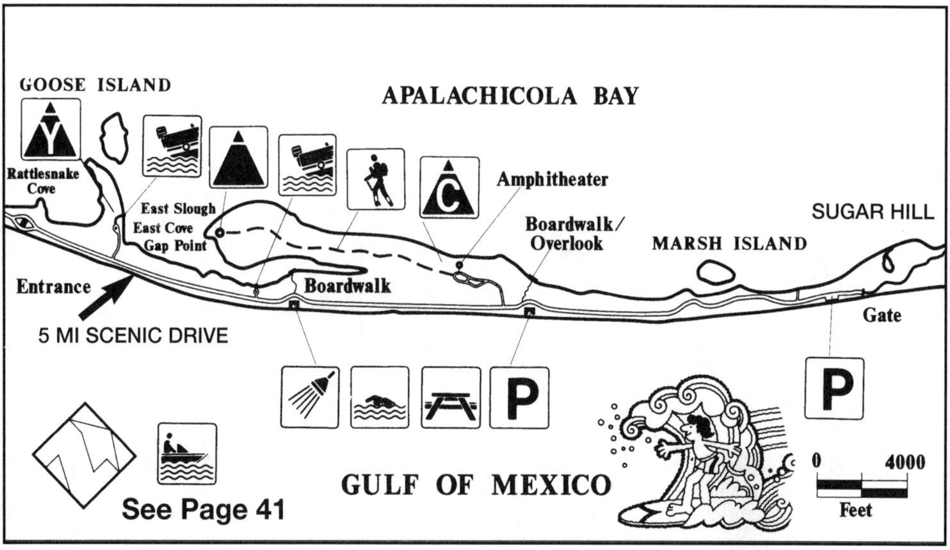

See Page 41

CAPE ST. GEORGE STATE PRESERVE

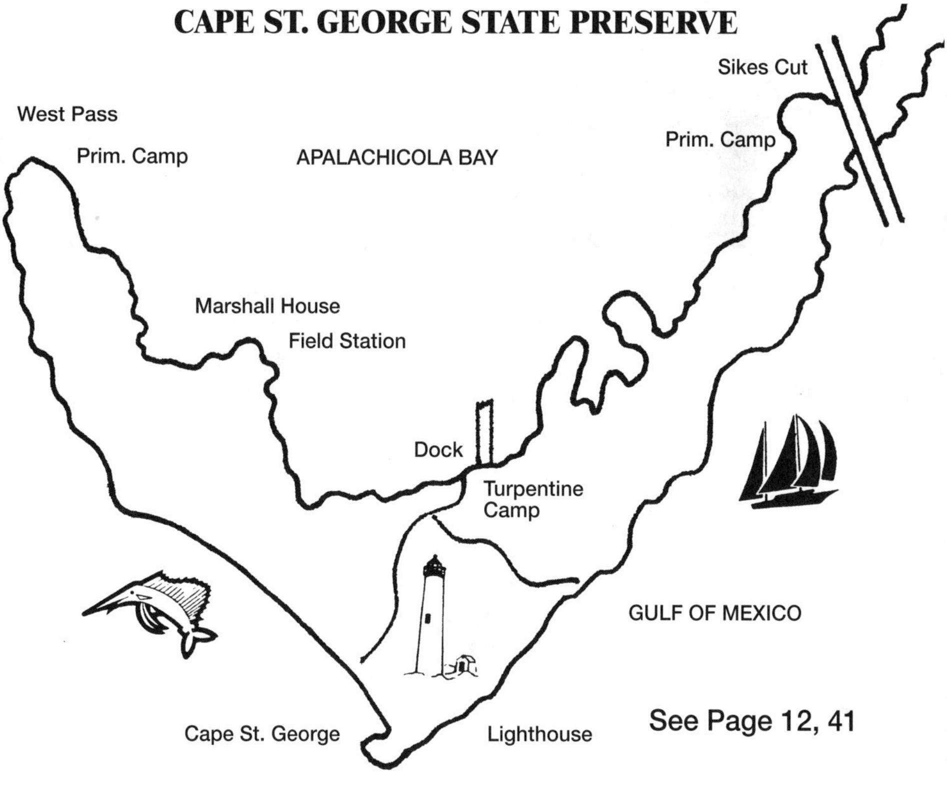

See Page 12, 41

APALACHEE SAVANNAHS SCENIC BYWAY

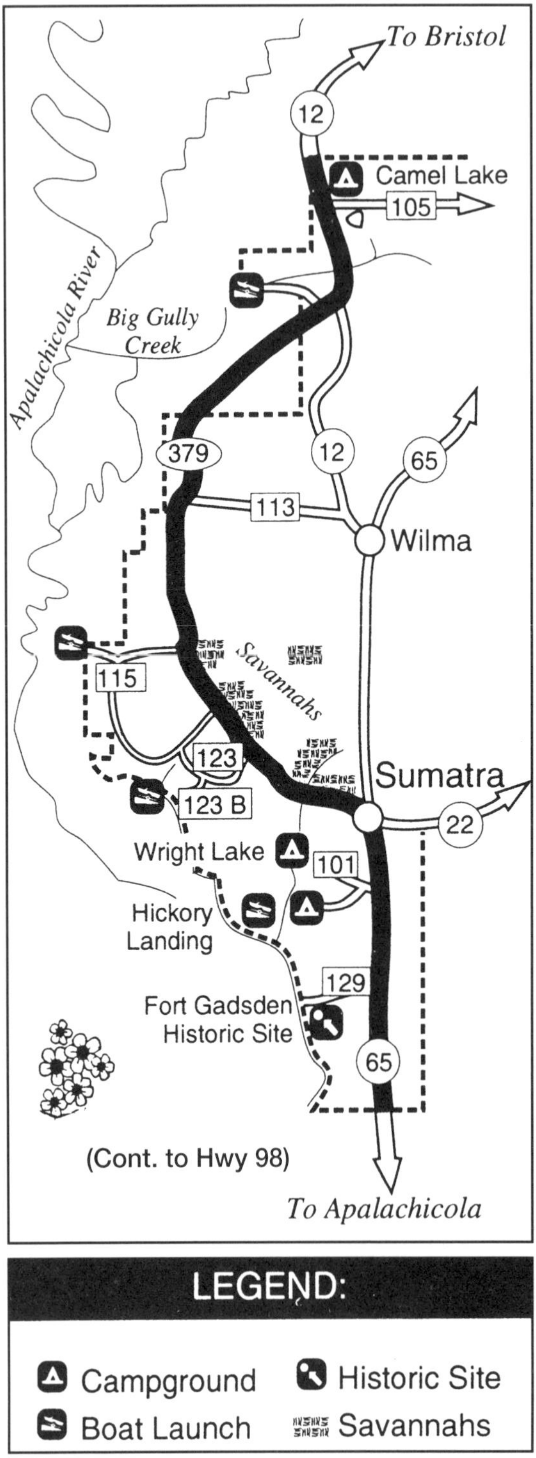

- Spring Wildflow Display
- Largest Block of Natural Wiregrass
- Magnolia and Cypress Bays
- Wright Lake Swimming

See Page 37

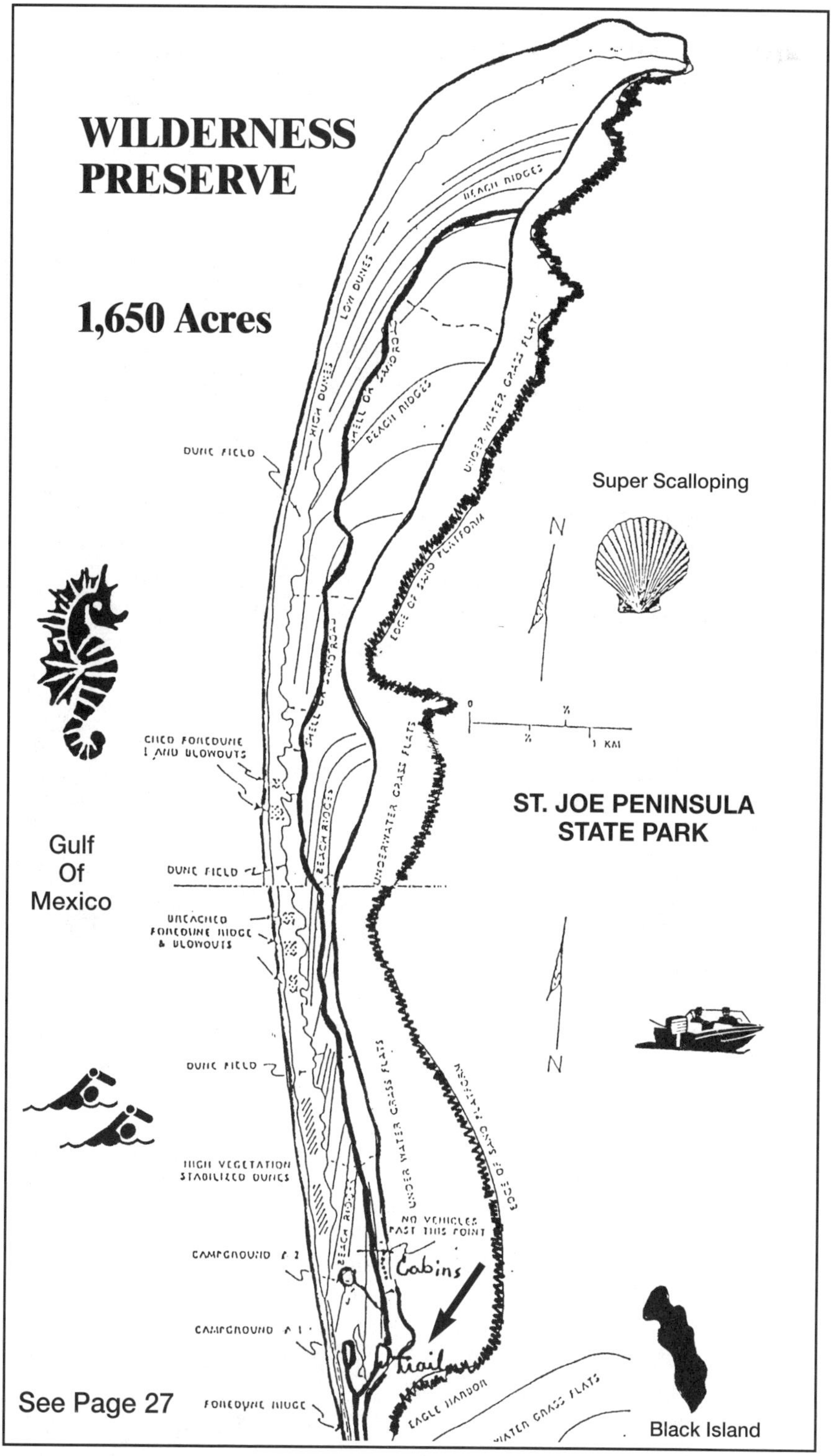

WILDERNESS PRESERVE
1,650 Acres
Super Scalloping
N
ST. JOE PENINSULA STATE PARK
Gulf Of Mexico
N
Cabins
Trail
See Page 27
Black Island

APALACHICOLA RIVER WILDLIFE-ENVIRONMENTAL AREA

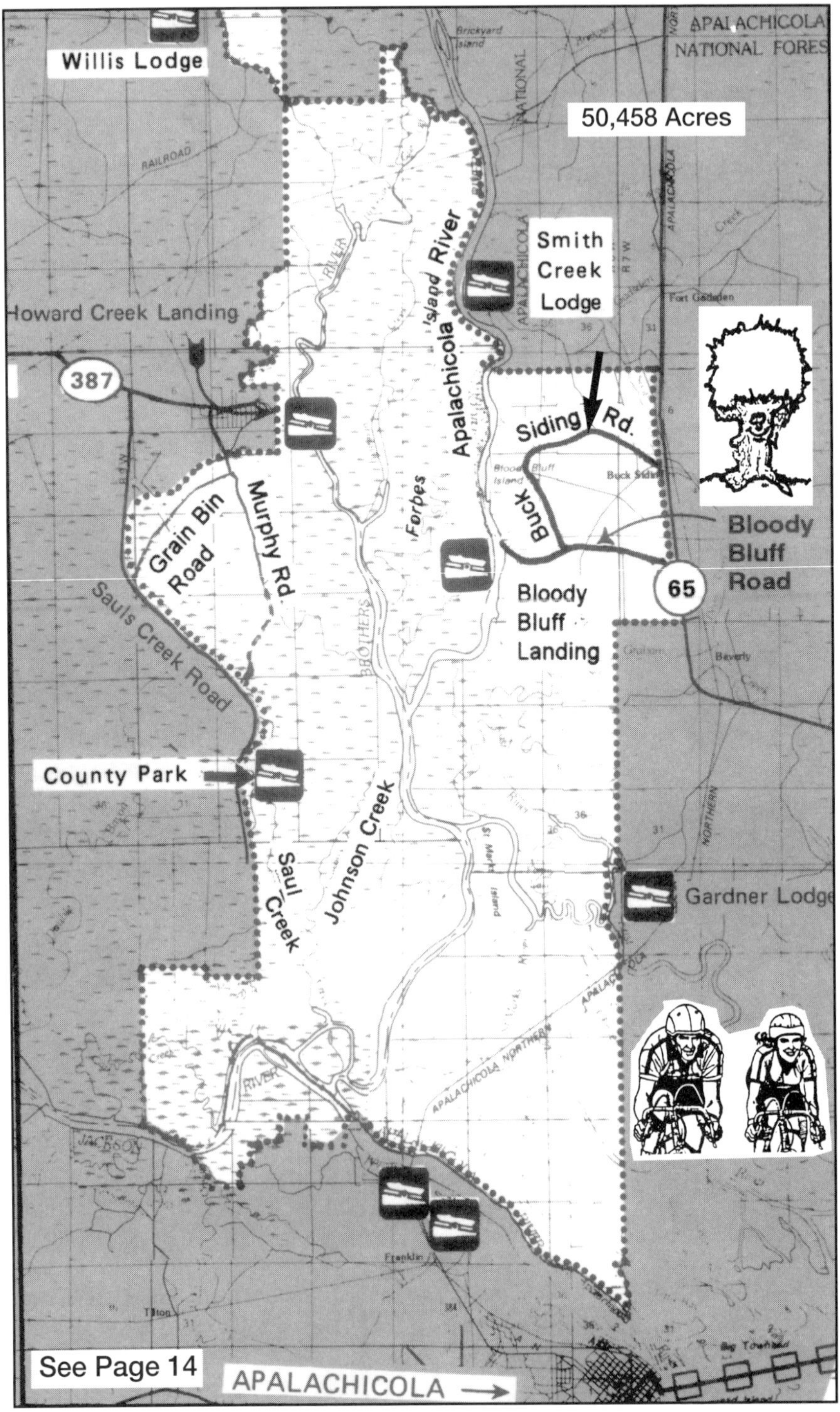

TATE'S HELL W.M.A. West Area

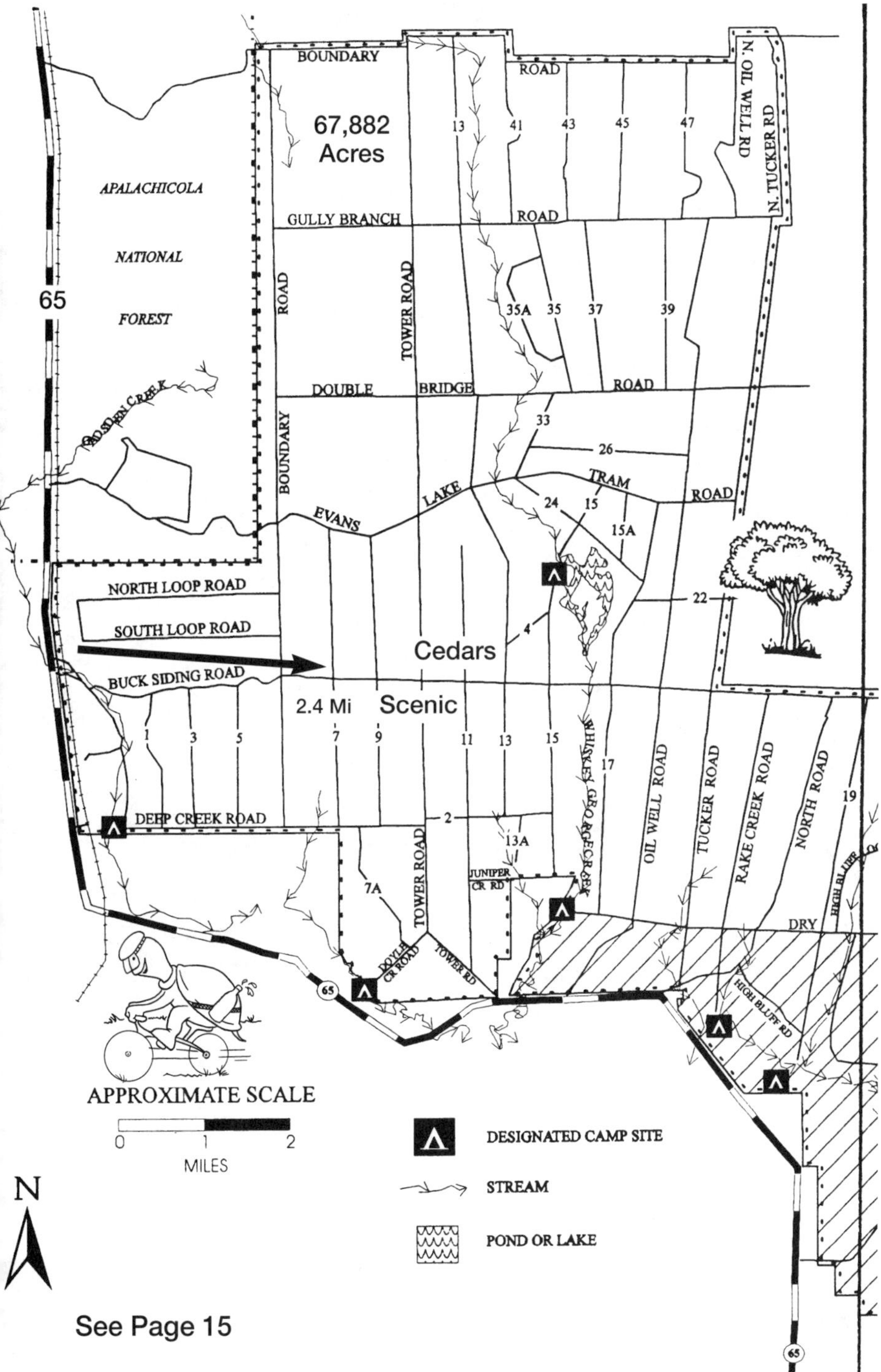

See Page 15

OLD STEAMBOAT LANDINGS
Apalachicola National Forest

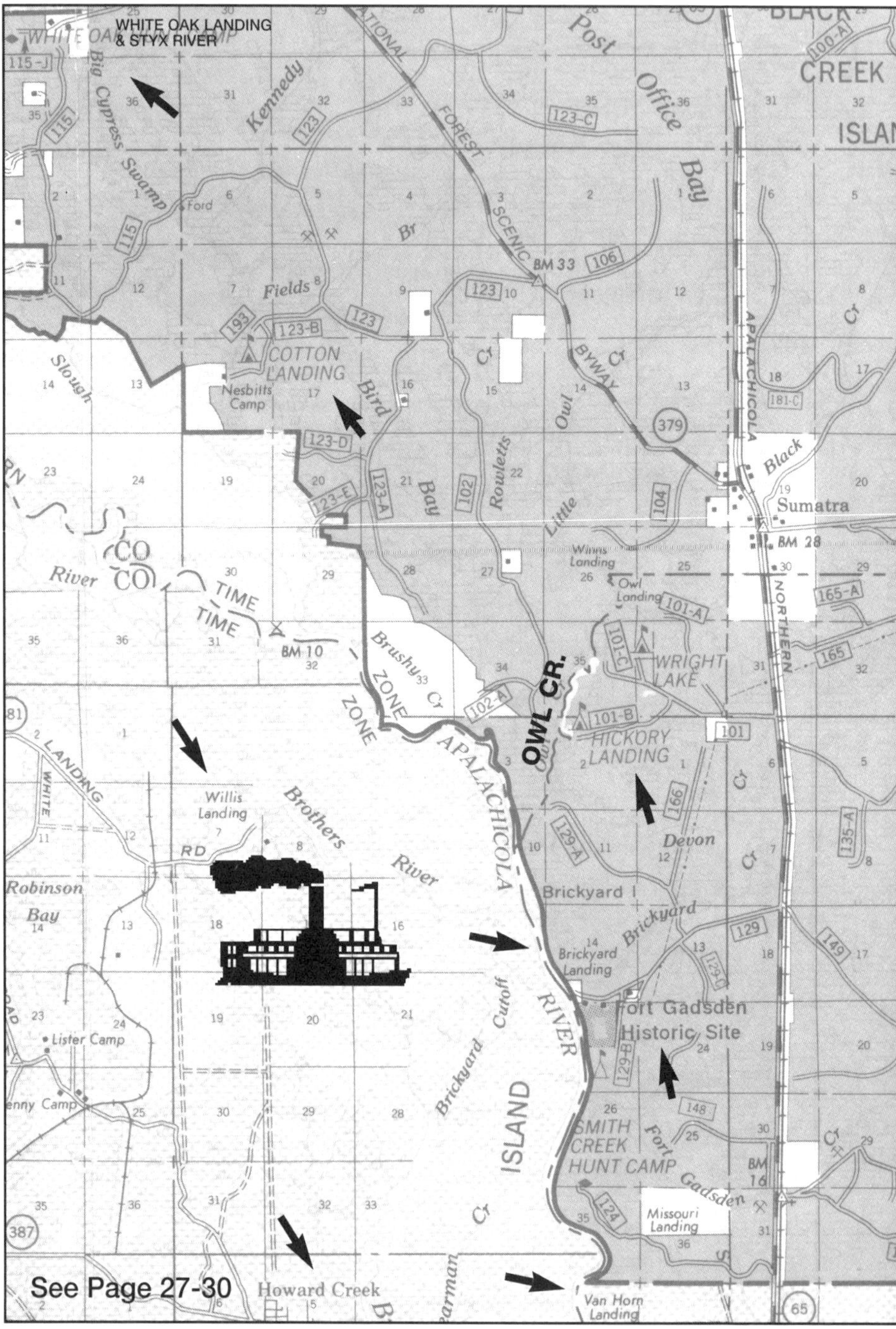

See Page 27-30

APALACHICOLA RIVER

LANDINGS AND MILEAGES

Apalachicola – John Gorrie Bridge, U.S. Highway 98	0.0
Big Townhead Island	0.3
Scipio Creek	0.6
Four Tree Cutoff	3.3
Poorhouse Creek & Bay City	3.5
Acorn Creek & Grassy Creek	4.4
Apalachicola Northern R.R. Bridge	4.5
Old Womans Bluff	5.0
Jackson River	5.9
Saul Creek Cutoff	6.2
Hoffman Creek at Hurricane Reach	8.0
Saint Marks River	10.2
Brothers River	12.0
Rangletts Bend	13.0
East River	13.9
Bloody Bluff Landing	14.5
Bloody Bluff Island	15.6
Van Horn Landing	16.3
Smith Creek	17.6
Fort Gadsden Creek	19.4
Fort Gadsden Landing	19.8
Hardee Landing	19.9
Marchant Landing	20.1
Patrick Landing	20.3
Brickyard Landing & Creek	20.6
Brickyard Cutoff	20.7
Brickyard Island	21.5
Owl Creek	22.2
Scott Creek	23.3
Brushy Creek	23.9
Kennedy Creek	26.0
Chipola River	27.9
Battle Bend Cutoff	28.8
River Styx	35.1
Tie Up Reach	37.5
Louisa Bend	38.6
Mocassin Slough	38.8
Flint Landing	41.3
Chipola Cutoff	41.5

Florida River 43.0
Kentucky Landing 43.7
Iola Landing 45.2
Porter Landing 48.2
Dicks Point 49.5
Brown Lake...........................49.5
Queen City Point 50.3
Gun Landing 54.1
Coons Landing 54.6
Iamonia Lake 55.8
Ricko Bluff 56.4
Standfield Landing..............58.6
Mosquito Landing 59.1
Muscogee Landing 60.3
Estiffanulga Landing...........63.5
Woods Landing 66.4
Hughes Landing 67.4
Bakers Landing 70.3
Riverside Landing 70.9
Poloway Cutoff....................71.3
Old River 72.9
Sheppard Landing...............75.6
Old River 76.6
Blounts Landing 77.3
Blountstown Bar 77.7
Suttons Lake 78.1
Calhoun Bridge,
State Highway 20 ....79.4

Ramsey Landing 80.2
Bristol Landing 80.4
Carter Landing 80.7
White Oak Landing 83.3
Alum Bluff 84.1
Little Sweetwater Creek.....84.2
Hollis Landing......................85.3
Porter's Landing..................88.2
Dawson Landing 89.6
Adkins Landing 90.2
Wayside Landing.................90.2
Caraway Landing 90.4
Rock Bluff Landing 92.2
Rock Bluff 92.2
Ocheesee Creek..................93.2
Coopers Landing.................94.7
Hickory Landing 97.7
Aspalaga Bluff 99.4
Aspalaga Creek...................99.5
I-10 Bridge 100.0
Coes Landing 100.0
Farrell Landing 103.0
L & N Railroad Bridge 104.9
U.S. Highway 90
Victory Bridge....................105.7
Jim Woodruff Lock............106.3